SKRIFTER FRA CENTER FOR RUSMIDDELFORSKNING

VOL. 2

T0108000

ALCOHOL AND DRUGS IN THE WORKPLACE

ATTITUDES, POLICIES, AND PROGRAMMES

IN DENMARK

Knud-Erik Sabroe

Country Report
for the
International Labour Office
in Collaboration with the
Commission of the European Communities

Aarhus 1994

INTRODUKTION

I forbindelse med sammenlægningen af de to tidligere forskningsenheder CANFAU og Københavnske Alkohol- og Narkotikaforskeres Samvirke under det nye navn Center for Rusmiddelforskning, blev det besluttet at videreføre CANFAU's hidtidige skriftserie under et nyt navn - **Skrifter fra Center for Rusmiddelforskning**. Det overordnede formål med skriftserien er stadig at fremme formidlingen af forskningsresultater inden for rusmiddelområdet.

Skriftseriens primære formål er således en præsentation af artikler af danske rusmiddelforskere, dog vil oversættelser af udenlandske forskeres artikler også kunne publiceres i skriftet. Redaktionen agter tillige at udgive engelsksprogede artikler af såvel danske som udenlandske forfattere. Som noget nyt vil skriftserien få et supplement, hvori bl.a. monografier vil blive publiceret.

Skriftserien redigeres af en redaktion, udpeget af medarbejderne ved centret, som inddrager ekstern redaktionel ekspertise fra et tværvidenskabeligt, tværnordisk sammensat redaktionspanel bestående af forskere tilknyttet rusmiddelområdet.

Skriftseriens enkelte numre vil bestå af artikelsamlinger. Skriftserien udgives ikke på faste tidspunkter, men når der forefindes relevante produkter, hvorfor redaktionen opfordrer forskere på rusmiddelområdet til at kontakte os vedrørende udgivelser af deres arbejder.

Redaktionen for dette nummer af skriftserien:

Mag. art. Karen Elmeland, Ph.D.
Dipl. Soz., lic. stip. Peter Nygaard

SKRIFTER FRA CENTER FOR RUSMIDDELFORSKNING

Copyright: Center for Rusmiddelforskning, Aarhus Universitet, Aarhus 1994

Sats: Marianne Bach Jacobsen

Tryk: Institut for Statskundskab, Aarhus Universitet

ISSN: 0909-9816
ISBN: 87-89029-14-3

Udgiver:

Center for Rusmiddelforskning
Tretommervej 1
8240 Risskov
86 17 80 44

Distribution:

Aarhus Universitetsforlag
Aarhus Universitet
8000 Århus C
86 19 70 33

FORORD

Denne publikation er den danske rapport i forbindelse med det af International Labour Office, Genève og EU-kommissionen DG V etablerede projekt "Alcohol and Drugs in the Workplace". Rapporten har været til diskussion i den samlede projektforskergruppe og til godkendelse i ILO/DG V og er nu frigivet med henblik på en national kommunikation af resultaterne. Rapporten vil indgå som bilag til en afsluttende publikation, der er planlagt færdiggjort med henblik på at skulle danne grundlag for et tre-parts møde i EU-regi, der afholdes i december 1995. Med henblik på dette vil rapporten til den tid foreligge i en dansk oversættelse fra EU-kommissionen.

Knud-Erik Sabroe, december 1994

Acknowledgement

The author wishes to express his thanks to all the representatives from enterprises, employer's and worker's organizations who volunteered to undertake the task of answering the lengthy questionnaire and participating in the interviews. The readiness whereby the request of participating in the project was received by almost all approached, was stimulating and indicated an experienced importance of and a concern for the subject.

Birthe Henriksen assisted in the administration of interview arrangements and typed the draft report. A great thank to her and Annie Dolmer Kristensen and Marianne Bach Jacobsen who made a fair copy of the final report, to Toke Sabroe who transcribed all the interviews from tapes, and to Rikke Jensen who helped with the data registration.

Contents

	page
Executive summary	1
I. Introduction	5
A. Background	5
B. Description of country situation	5
1. Demographic information.	5
2. Economy	8
3. Labour market relations	9
C. Methods	13
1. Criteria of selection of participants	13
2. Population	13
3. Administration of questionnaire and interviews	15
4. Analysis of data	16
5. Validity and reliability of results	17
II. Nature, extent and trends in alcohol and drug problems in the workplace	19
A. Introduction	19
B. Alcohol consumption	19
C. Danish alcohol policy	23
D. Alcohol-related problems	25
E. Danish drug policy	28
F. Research on alcohol and drugs in the workplace	30
G. Frequency of alcohol and drug-related problems	33
H. Attitudes towards the nature of the problem	36
III. Policy and organizational aspects	39
A. General background	39

    B. Alcohol, drugs and the workplace 40

    C. Views and attitudes from enterprises and

        organizations 42

    D. Attitudes towards treatment of alcohol and drug

        problems 43

IV. Worker - employer relations 45

V. Programmes in response to problems 47

    A. Overview 47

    B. Organizations and alcohol programmes 48

    C. Enterprises and alcohol programmes 48

    D. Information and availability of assistance 49

    E. Drug programmes 51

VI. Cost of the problem and cost of responses 53

VII. Drug and alcohol testing and screening 55

VIII.Information availability and exchange 57

IX. Outlook and opinion 59

References 63

Annex one: The transport sector. A profile 67

Annex two: Alcohol patterns of the Danish population 73

    Figure 1: Alcohol consumption (in total) 74

    Figure 2: Average amount consumed over 24 hours 74

Figure 3: Consumption distribution (types of alcohol)
over 24 hours 75

Figure 4: Consumption according to day of week 76

Figure 5: Consumption distribution (type of alcohol)
over the week 77

Figure 6: Alcohol consumption (gender) over 24 hours 78

Figure 7: Alcohol consumption according to age 79

Annex three: Data on alcohol and work 81

Table 1: Alcohol consumption in the workplace 81

Table 2: Alcohol consumption in the workplace according to age   82

Table 3: Alcohol consumption in the workplace according
to occupation 82

Table 4: Access to alcohol in the workplace 83

Table 5: Work colleagues with a high alcohol consumption 83

Annex four: Tables from national report on the drug abuse situation 85

Table 1: Seizures of drugs 1986-1989 85

Table 2: Charges of drug related crime 85

Table 3: Percentage of adults tried drugs 86

Table 4: Drugs and treatment 86

Table 5: Drugs and death 86

Annex five: Alcohol related problems. Health statistics 87

Table 1: Treatment in wards and alcohol clinics 87

Table 2: Alcohol related deaths 87

Table 3: Alcohol and traffic 88

Annex six: Facts on alcohol and drug misuse in Denmark 89

Annex seven: English resume of Danish Health council
sheet on Alcohol and work 91

List of tables in the report:

Table 1:   Employed population by sector   10

Table 2:   Enterprises. Distribution according to size   10

Table 3:   Average consumption in 100% alcohol (> 14 years)   21

Table 4:   Distribution of type of beverages consumed   22

Table 5:   Drug experimentation and use   29

Table 6:   Attitude to prohibition of alcohol in the workplace

according to average level of drinking   32

Table 7:   Frequency of alcohol and drug related work problems

(enterprises)   34

Table 8:   Frequency of alcohol and drug related work problems

(organizations)   35

Table 9:   Level of concern regarding alcohol and drug use as

potential causes of work-related problems   36

Table 10: Increase/decrease in problems with alcohol or drugs   36

Table 11: Attitudes towards the nature of alcohol and drug problems   37

Table 12: Responses to employees with alcohol or other drug problems..   42

Table 13: Time of introduction of policies   43

Table 14: Attitudes towards treatment   44

Table 15: Views on reactions to alcohol and drug problems   46

Table 16: Information and training provided by enterprises   49

Table 17: Internal resources for alcohol and drug

prevention/treatment   50

Table 18: External resources for alcohol and drug prevention/treatment   50

Table 19: Attitude to testing/screening. Enterprises and organizations ...   56

Table 20: Information topics ranked by organizations and enterprises ...   57

Executive summary

Sabroe, Knud-Erik (1993). *Alcohol and drugs in the workplace: Attitudes, policies and programmes in Denmark.* Aarhus: Institute of Psychology. (Country report for the International Labour Office in collaboration with Commission of the European Communities).

If the major message of the country report of Denmark should be summed up in one sentence, a misquotation could be used of Marcellus' line from the first act of *Hamlet*: "*Something is changing in the state of Denmark*". Taken by its wording, one could, of course, say that this is a triviality, for naturally something is always changing. But if you add the qualification of the line that the change is to the better, the statement goes beyond the trivial. So what is this change?

The dominant impression is that within the last 3-4 years a change in attitudes has moved the topic of alcohol in the workplace from being a *conflictual* topic between employers and employees to be one of *common concern*. In the same process the culture-dominant *tabooing* of drink problems among management and employee has been attacked. On this general founding specific efforts have been initiated. Among these are the publishing of a joint recommendation from the *Danish Confederation of Trade Unions* and the *Danish Employers' Confederation* to establish alcohol policy in the enterprises, an increase in the percentage of Danish enterprises establishing an alcohol policy, the inclusion of alcohol and work as a topic in the national campaigns, greater concern from the county-authorities regarding support for prevention in the workplace.

Something that is not changing is the average consumption of alcohol. From a decline in the late eighties, a stabilization seemed to be the trend in the first 2 years of the nineties, but the last figures have shown a rise.

The situation regarding illicit drugs is not regarded as a workplace problem in Denmark, concern being expressed, however, of the development in general in the country.

The main results of the investigation are summed up in seven points below representing *ten* organizations and *seven* enterprises. They are formulated in "*agreement terms*". This is felt substantiated by the results, of course, but it is necessary to say that there are differences in opinions across the organizations and enterprises. The differences regarding the central matters could be said to be exceptions compared to the agreements, however. When used below the word "agreement" should thus be interpreted as covering a clear majority view.

1. There is an agreement that in general the level of alcohol consumption in Denmark is high, and that illegal drug is an existing problem, confined to marginal groups, however. Further that the general consumption of prescribed drugs is relatively high.

2. There is an agreement that the actual incidence of workplace problems related to alcohol are low and to drugs extremely low. There is, nevertheless, somewhat concern about the alcohol situation and for the prescribed drug situation a feeling of uncertainty. Illegal drug as a workplace problem is considered extremely small verging on non-existing.

3. There is an agreement that alcohol and drug policies in the workplace are a good thing, that they, if not yet introduced, should be established through negotiations between employers and employees, and that these negotiations in general have been or will be successful.

4. There is an agreement that prevention of alcohol/drug related work problems should be given high priority.

5. There is an agreement that a case to case approach should be used when problems appear based on individual circumstances.

6. There is an agreement that testing and screening, as defined in the project, in general are incompatible with the Danish attitude to the individual and his/her integrity. When asked about practical aspects there is an opinion that incidences anyway are too small to justify testing, and that testing is too costly.

7. There is an agreement that the enterprise has the responsibility to support treatment and rehabilitation of employees if they run into troubles, and at the same time a belief that employees respond well to management and/or treatment.

To characterize the seven points above as the general picture of the Danish workplace is maybe *too* audacious. The participants in the investigation are *not* representative, though especially on the organizations' side there is a broad covering. A factor of importance is that the area of small and medium size enterprises is uncovered in the investigation, and the problem of reaching this major part of the Danish labour market must be the basis for thorough thinking. But, on the other hand, the obtained results display a consistency, have an inborn logic and are in accordance with other knowledge. They should therefore at least be regarded as a straw in the wind and a foundation for further action.

Introduction

A.   Background

In response to growing European interest in drug and alcohol problems in the workplace, this project is designed to increase the understanding of: (a) the nature of these problems in the 12 countries of the E.C. and (b) the attitudes, policies and programmes developed in these countries to prevent problems and assist those workers who need it. With support from the Commission of the European Communities, this project is sponsored by the International Labour Office for the immediate objective of improved knowledge and capability to prevent problems and assist workers.

Based on guidelines and procedures prepared by the ILO, collaborators in each country will facilitate this project by providing advice, gathering information, and preparing reports. Criteria for selection of enterprises, employer's and worker's organisations have been developed and instruments prepared to gather information. Collaborators will prepare country reports addressing a variety of topics such as: the nature of workplace drug and alcohol problems and their seriousness; policies; the impact of problems on employer and employee relations; programmes including planning, prevention, treatment, and rehabilitation; costs; beliefs about alcohol and drugs; testing and screening; availability and exchange of information; and, outlook and opinion.

Using the country reports and other sources, the ILO will prepare a synthetic international paper examining the situation in the Community. Legal and policy aspects of drugs and alcohol will be considered in a separate but related study carried out by a legal expert. Country collaborators will meet in two workshops: one on methods and the other reviewing information and country reports. These workshops will insure peer review of the approach and the results obtained, and the direct exchange of information among the collaborators. A directory of information and education resources on this subject will be prepared to facilitate the exchange of information on a broad basis throughout the Community.

B.   Description of country situation

1. Demographic Information

Denmark (population a. 5 millions) is a constitutional *monarchy* with a *one chamber* parliamentary system and universal suffrage from the age of eighteen, elections taking place at three levels, national ("Folketinget"), regional ("Amtsråd") and local ("Byråd" or "Kommunalbestyrelser"). The three sectors *social, education* and *health* constitutes the major part of the national budget, covering 40, 12 and 9% respectively. Taxation is heavy as are the excise duties. By 1992 Denmark is having the highest tax burden of all OECD countries. Prices on alcohol and tobacco are among the highest in Europe. Reductions of excises have taken place during the last couple of years, however, because of problems with the border trade across the Danish-German border. In addition there is a value-added tax (VAT) of 25% on all goods and services. This compiled tax burden is the price for living in a *welfare society* with very high social and health security and equal opportunity for all to obtain the highest educational levels.

The civil service is structured at three levels: *government* level, *county* level and *municipality* level. Counties on the average comprise about 300.000 persons. Municipalities of course vary a lot, one level being the capital (with over the million inhabitants) and three greater provincial cities (200.000-300.000), another being medium seized towns, and the third level small seized municipalities being on the average about 18.000 inhabitants. There is to a great extent autonomy at the regional and local level. The Parliament establishes statues through legislation which define the economical and administrative responsibilities of the regions and municipalities. Autonomy means in this connection that the government cannot intervene in the local government outside of what is stated in the statues from the Parliament.

The economical foundation for central and local government is taxes. Levy of taxes takes place at all three levels. The level of taxation at county and municipality level is decided locally though the government can ask the local government e.g. to keep increase of taxation within certain limits, in consideration of the total tax load. The government provides bloc grants, which are determined according to the structure and character of the local area and which function as a supplement to locally levied taxes.

There are 14 counties and 275 municipalities, the counties being chiefly responsible for the *health sector* covering about 75% of the total health expenditures in the country, whereas the municipalities bear the main burden of social sector outlay currently at about 80% of the total social expenses. The major part of *educational sector* outlays is divided with about 40% to the state (mainly higher education including research) and just over 50% to the municipalities.

6

Compulsory *school attendance* is nine years but about 37% of the pupils continue and take a further three years leading up to the university or higher education entrance level. All school attendance is free and covered through taxes; the same applies for vocational training and higher education. A minor part of the schoolchildren (11%) attend private schools, these being of diverse origin from a religious through a specific pedagogical to a grassroot basis. The state covers 85% of the expenses for these schools, however.

The *health system* provides equal and free access to both general practice services, hospitals and various special health services. The health system is built up around the general practitioner (G.P.), and in general hospitalization demands that one is referred through a G.P.. The G.P.'s are however solely engaged as a family doctor and have no attachment to the public hospitals. During the last 4-5 years private hospitals have been introduced in Denmark (especially though not exclusively geared towards surgery). Here it is possible to get a treatment, paying the expenses, that you would otherwise have had to wait for due to waiting lists in the public system. At present they constitute a very minor part of the health system, but their presence is also being felt in the treatment of alcoholism and drug addiction, in particular through the formation of so-called "Minnesota-model" clinics. Here it is not as much a waiting list problem as an attempt at establishing an alternative to the public treatment possibilities. The public treatment is to the major extent built on the assumption that alcohol related problems are multi-caused and aims at controlled drinking. Many alternative clinics are based on the assumption that alcohol-dependence is a disease, and nothing but total abstinence is a way to handle it.

As already mentioned *social security* is high. Especially the Law of Un-employment Aid and the General Aid Law ensure that people in unfortunate cir-cumstances are able to sustain a reasonable standard of living, the idea being that he/she will not be forced to undertake drastic alteration in the daily life in the hopefully short period the person is unemployed or suffering from other social mishaps.

The *training* of health personnel as well as social sector employees at professional and subprofessional level is a state responsibility. This is also the case for the licensing of health personnel. *Medicine* is a six years university study in Denmark and *psychology* are five years of study at the university. *Nurses* and *social workers* have a three year education in schools outside the university.

2. Economy

Denmark through a referendum decided to join the European Communities in 1973. A major characteristic through the last decade has been a varying deficit at the national budget, peaking in 1983. The later years have showed a tendency to go in black figures. The inflation rate has been low (a. 3%) throughout this period, while the unemployment rate has been rising being, in 1992 approximately 10%. Denmark has experienced a growth of its economy and of the labour force for a major period of the eighties and the early nineties, two major recessions appearing in 1982 and 1987, however. But the repercussions of the situation until recently - that Denmark had to import seventy-five percent of its energy need - have caused the structural problem of a major deficit in the balance of payments. This deficit is to a high degree in the last four to five years caused by the burden of interest of the great loans taken up abroad to cover the deficit of the state budget which rose in the period from 1975 to 1985 topping in 1983 with 54 billion Danish kroner (equals to 6.8 billion ECU).

Denmark as a producer of alcohol and medicine/pharmaceuticals

Alcohol

Denmark has a production of beer, spirits and fortified wine. The last two on the basis of other products than grapes. The greatest production is of beer which amounts to about 8,500.000 hl per year of which about 30% is exported. Import of beer corresponds to roughly 0.4% of the total beer consumption. Spirits as well as fortified wines are exported but for these two types of alcohol the major part also goes to the home market (70% of the total production). Denmark imports alcoholic beverages for 2,018 million Danish kroner and exports to the amount of 1,589 million Danish kroner (1993 figures).

Pharmaceuticals (prescribed drugs)

A medicine industry exists in Denmark and one of the enterprises are internationally seen at a rather high level. Psychoactive drugs are not among the main products of the industry, however. Denmark imports medicine and other pharmaceuticals for approx. 4,000 million Danish kroner and exports to the amount of 10,000 million Danish kroner (1992 figures).

3. Labour Market Relations

The Danish Labour Force

The Danish labour force comprises approx. three million of which 54% are men, 46% women. The percentage of women being part of the labour force has been rising over the last four-five decades and is now one of the highest in Europe with nearly 78% (Danmarks Statistik, 1994).

The average working hours are 37 hours a week. But in some areas, especially in the public sector, one find a considerable burden of overtime. For all sectors the figure for men is 26%, for women 10% with working hours above 39 hours a week (Bunnage, 1992). Parttime working has been slightly declining for women, in the same period, and slightly rising for men: 11% men and 35% women work less than 30 hours a week.

An essential problem is a very high degree of moonlightning, an amount having resulted in establishing of national and local campaigns to "stop it".

The distribution regarding occupational groups is: salaried employees 44%; unskilled workers 18%; skilled workers 10%; self-employed 9%; non-specified 9% and unemployed 10%. The women have a 3% higher unemployment rate than men. Highest unemployment is among workers in their twenties, lowest among those in their forties.

The distribution according to industrial sector is shown in table 1:

Table 1: Employed population by sector

Sector	Approx. percentage
Manufacturing	20%
Social and health services	16%
Financing	9%
Public services, general administration	9%
Retail trade	8%
Transport	8%
Education and research	8%
Wholesale trade	7%
Construction and building	6%
Other services	5%
Restaurants and hotels	3%
Electricity, gas, water, mining	0.6%
Not stated	0.4%

In table 2 is shown the distribution of enterprises according to size. As seen, more than 80% of the enterprises are small (<50 employees) and 50% even have less than 20 employees.

Table 2: Enterprises. Distribution according to size

Number of employees	Approx. Percentage
<9	18%
10-19	32%
20-49	31%
50-99	13%
>100	6%

(Source: Statistisk Årbog, 1992)

Agreements

For nearly a hundred years the relations between the parties at the labour market have been regulated according to a so-called "Hovedaftale" (Main Agreement), the first being approved in September 1899. This Main Agreement includes two major issues, one being rules for conflict (workers' right to strike and employers' right of lock-out). The right to use conflict though is only accepted in the formal negotiation's period, between these an embargo is in force. The other important issue is the provision that the employer has the right to supervise and distribute the work, and the workers the right to organize themselves in unions.

The actual agreements of wages and working conditions are laid down in a collective settlement between workers' (and salaried employees/civil servants), organizations and employers' organizations (which also could be confederation of municipalities and counties and the State).

The State has established an official mediator institution for the labour market. If the parties decide that an agreement cannot be reached within the given period, the official mediator will join the negotiations and has the power to postpone a strike or lock-out. The official mediator has the possibility to present the parties a draft of compromise. If mediating doesn't succeed, the government can interfere and establish wages and working conditions by law. If doing so, the official mediator's draft of compromise is often used as the law text.

Offences against or disputes about the interpretation of the Main Agreement or other collective agreements can be brought before the labour court (industrial relations court). This institution has a juridical chairman and vice-chairmen (with judge appointments) and 12 lay judges appointed by the employers' and workers' organizations, the salaried workers' organization, the ministries and local authorities' organizations.

Denmark has been free of major labour market unrest for a rather long period, and through the later years a moving has taken place from placing wages in the centre of negotiations to give priority to working conditions and welfare. This might have eased the way for taking up problems as attitudes to alcohol and drugs at the workplace.

Organization

Denmark is regarded generally as one of the most thoroughly organized countries in the world (by interest groups). This also counts for the labour market. More than 85% of the wage-earners are members of a union and the percentage of employers being member of an employer's organization is high, also.

The labour market is organized through the existence of some major umbrella organizations in industry, agriculture and trade being the Danish Confederation of Trade Unions (with about 1.4 million members) and Danish Employer's Confederation (organizing enterprises with about 1 million workers). In the public sector it is Federation of Civil Servants and Salaried Employees' Organizations (about 300.000 members) and the Federation of Academics (about 100.000 members). The last two mentioned organizations having mainly the State and the Federation of Municipalities/Counties as their negotiation partners.

The Danish Confederation of Trade Unions has very strong relations with the Social-Democrat Party, and to a certain degree The Employer's Confederation is connected with the Conservatives Party. The two wage-earner organizations, mainly oriented towards the public sector, are considered to be politically neutral.

By tradition the Danish worker has been organized in unions according to trade. In a workplace workers could be members of several unions thus. In general skilled and unskilled workers belong to separate unions and a special feature for Denmark is, that all unskilled workers are organized in two major organizations: The National Union of General Workers and the Female Worker's Confederation (both of course being members of the umbrella organization mentioned above). For many years and especially intensive from the early eighties the worker's organizations have discussed another structure, however, organizing workers according to the branch of trade (type of industry), in which they work. In 1987 a proposal was submitted at the congress of the Confederation of Trade Unions suggesting an organization in eight to ten branch-cartels. A general agreement was not obtained, however, mainly due to opposition from the General Worker's and Female Worker's organization. In certain areas cartels have been established, though. At the employer side similar thoughts of going together in branch related amalgamations have existed and some have been established.

At the enterprise level two bodies are - by law - established to deal with problems between employers and workers. The management of the enterprises is responsible for the establishment of the two bodies and have the chair. The number of members is uneven and the employer's representative can never outnumber the worker's representatives. The opposite is permitted, however. One body is the Joint Industrial Council taking care of all general aspects of working life the other is the Security Committee which deals with matters related to all types of risk situations at the workplace solely. At the enterprise level the question of alcohol and drugs in the workplace will be dealt with in the Joint Industrial Council, normally.

C. Methods

1. Criteria of selection of participants

As stated in the background description (p. 4), the overall purpose of the project was to establish a foundation and facilitate the exchange of information regarding alcohol and drugs in the workplace. Following this intent, a study was set up seeking systematic knowledge regarding the nature of eventual problems in the EC countries, of assistance and prevention programmes in the workplace and of underlying attitudes and policies.

Common data collection instruments were established by ILO/CEC in co-operation with the country collaborators being a questionnaire and an interview guide specific devised (though greatly overlapping) for enterprises and for worker's and employer's organizations. The employment of these instruments were designed to be flexible in order that as well direct contact (single interviews, telephone or face to face; group interviews) as postal survey techniques could be used.

Being small and having a highly organized labour market, Denmark is a country making it possible to have face to face interviews with persons having responsibility for the alcohol/drug area at the highest possible position in central organizations and to have the same persons to fill out the questionnaire. Regarding enterprises the choice was to include enterprises of which it was known that the problem in some way or other had been dealt with, seeking to have a spread and to consider the transport sector, though (pointed out as a priority area by ILO/CEC).

2. Population

Ten organizations at employer and employee level (representing about 2 million employees) and seven enterprises (with a total of approx. 49.000 employees) constituted the participants from Denmark.

Regarding organizations there was a coverage of the major part of the labour market. In relation to workers and salaried employees organizations at the confederation level, at the branch of trade level and at occupation level were part of the population. From employers participated organizations at the

13

confederation level, at sector level and at branch level. The organizations chosen represented a cross section of the labour market including skilled and unskilled workers, salaried employees and civil servants.

Danish industry and trade as well as the service sector are characterized by relatively few large enterprises, meaning that middle size and especially relatively small size enterprises (less than 25 employees) are the major types (cf. p. 9). Choosing enterprises for the project it was decided to go for relatively big enterprises, though, based on a knowledge indicating that alcohol policy discussions until recently had been taken up in bigger enterprises mainly. The size of enterprises entering the project is from about 600 to 21,000 employees. But as mentioned on p. 2 serious thougths must be given as to the way of obtaining data regarding the situation in the small-medium sized enterprises and the evaluation of the way an alcohol and drug policy could be part of the culture of this major part of the labour market.

In general the request of participating in the project was received positively by as well organizations as enterprises. Previously to sending the formal request from ILO, contacts were taken by personal phone calls to the highest level of the organizations/enterprises considered responsible for alcohol and drug questions. This preliminary contact established a provisional agreement of participating in the project. Two of the organizations contacted declined to participate, one verbally arguing that the problem had not been discussed at the organizational level, and no organizational action taken or planned. The other organization (a major organization in the sector of civil servants and salaried employees) gave a written explanation stating that they found method and instruments of low scientific standard (!) and claiming that they had negative experiences with previous participation in surveys from "Brussels" (!). In two cases enterprises contacted declined to participate. In one case the reason given by a major company was a company decision not to participate in investigations, but information was volunteered, that the company had an alcohol prohibition policy (drug was considered a non-existent problem) and the employee observed the rules, one reason maybe being that the jobs in the company were much coveted. In the other case the reason given was that the company had in agreement established an alcohol policy after rather difficult negotiations in the company's joint industrial council, and they did not want a participation in the project to give cause for unrest.

3. Administration of questionnaire and interviews

The questionnaire was sent to the participants in beforehand. In a few cases it was answered previous to the interview. But in the majority of the cases, the questionnaire had been looked through, and the occasion was taken to give comments in connection with the interviewing. Some of the participants also wanted to have the interview-guide sent in advance of the interview.

The main content of the comments on the questionnaire was, that many of the questions were found difficult to answer in a concrete way because of their often very broad scope and abstractness, and that it was rather awkward sometimes to be forced to react on the basis of impressions and assumptions. Similar reactions were received in relation to the interview guide, but in the interview situation one forwarded the information asked for in an appropriate way nevertheless.

Some general comments seemed to stand out from the individual participants. Regarding the *interview guide* the above mentioned problems with the content and broadness of the questions and the difficulties in answering them were most frequent. This problem was more often indicated by representatives of employer or worker organizations than by the enterprise representatives.

In relation to the *questionnaire* three major reactions were dominant, presented both by organizations and enterprises: (1) Taking alcohol and drugs together into questions gave an inconvenient interference between the two when answering - especially from drugs on alcohol. (2) Some of the questions were formulated in such a way that they were experienced guiding, for example in the section on testing. (3) Some of the questions were experienced as based on pre-determined suppositions. Examples were questions, that seemed to presuppose that alcohol-work was a subject that would cause conflicts between employer and employees establishing alcohol policies etc. Several of the participants also had comments regarding the scaling of questionnaire responses. One comment was that it was difficult to interpret the meaning "unknown" and the other was that "sometimes" gave too broad a possibility for interpretation and was not a good "medium term" between "never" and "often".

It is an impression from talks around these problems between the national project coordinator and the participants, however, that the problems having been discussed with the coordinator, the objections voiced by participants were "disregarded" and only to a minor degree influenced the interviewing and questionnaire answering.

The interviewing was in all cases undertaken by the project-co-ordinator. The interviews took place in an office or meeting room at the enterprises or organizations headquarters. The interview situation took place in a positive and relaxed atmosphere, most often over a cup of coffee in some cases followed by a lunch. In nearly all cases there were a broader discussion after the interview relating to labour market policy in general, working conditions in general, topics of which the project coordinator was thought to have special knowledge (psychology), EC problems and so on. All interviews were taped; about one third of the participants wanted assurance of anonymity before accepting the taping.

It was very difficult to establish interview situations with a (small) group participation as intended. In most cases the organizations, when contacted, referred the dealing with the project to the working conditions and environment department and these in most cases decided that a single or two persons should represent the organization. Reasons given were that attitudes related to alcohol and drugs in the workplace were included in the general organizational policy and therefore could be expressed by a single representative. In some cases a pre-talk took place in which participated one or two other persons, but these persons did not participate in the interview. In three of the accomplished interviews with organizations more than one person participated. The reactions regarding questionnaires were along similar lines. It was argued that opinions stated would be of "political decision" character, and one questionnaire answered therefore would represent the views in general.

The reactions from enterprises were similar. Only in one case the managing director and the personnel director were jointly interviewed, in two other cases the managing director were present in a pre-talk, while the interview as in the rest of the cases were undertaken with the personnel director responsible for the alcohol (and drug) policy. From enterprises it also was argued that one questionnaire expressed "the views of the enterprise" suficiently.

4. Analysis of Data

For all participants in the investigation, two sets of data were obtained, a questionnaire and an interview. All interviews were taped and transcribed afterwards. In analysing the data, the questionnaire data were used as the foundation and supplied with the qualitative data from the interviews. No

16

statistical testing was used owing to the relatively small number of cases and consequently results are expressed in (qualified) impressions and experienced tendencies to a high degree, this in accordance with the exploratory character of the study. Neither was used tests to calculate differences between the different sectors represented in the investigation or between the different unions. One exception is that in a supplement a special attention is paid to the transport sector, trying to provide a profile of this sector using enterprises and organizations connected with it and participating in the project.

5. Validity and reliability of the results

Some aspects of this problem have already been touched upon above. But one of the problems concerning the data is the size of the population of course. In spite of the fact that some of the largest organizations participated in the investigation representing the workers' and employers' side both, thus "covering" the major part of the labour market. It was a single or at the most two persons from each organization who answered the questionnaire or were interviewed. It was stressed in the preliminary talks leading up to accepting the participation, however, that an organizational view was wanted and that the participant was in a position to express this view. It is our impression that several of these interviewed had conferred their organization's position before entering the interview/questionnaire situation. It was a general trait for nearly all organization interviews that the personal pronoun used by the interviewee was "we" and not "I". Calculating significant differences must, of course, be out of the question and a more qualitative analysis and interpretation employed as well for the questionnaire as for the interview data.

On factor of importance is the cultural differences caused by the use of the English language in the basic material (questionnaire and interview guide) and the primarily anglo saxon orientation of it. One problem is, for example, that drug is not used in Danish language as a joint term, but must be given as at least two independent terms. Another is that in Danish language one often express normal consumption of alcohol as - literally translated - "enjoying alcohol" (cf. also German and Dutch). A third factor is the difference between the implicit understanding of the organization of the labour market laid down in the questions and the Danish organizing. Wonder was often expressed over the questions raised. Fourthly - especially related to the testing - it was difficult to raise these questions at all. As the all dominant attitude in the Danish Parliament and at the labour market is one against testing the reaction from the respondents sometimes were: "How can you raise such questions at all?" It is a problem thus that a double process of translating questions from English to

Danish and the answers of these questions from Danish to English has to be carried out. The risk of loss of genuine meanings and cultural characteristics is present.

As stated above, the design of the study does not allow statistically documented generalizations. But the results nevertheless provide a picture that should be considered valid. The consistency by which uniform reactions to crucial questions appear across the different organizations and enterprises and their coherence with knowledge obtained through other sources indicate that a valid knowledge has been obtained.

II. Nature extent and trends in alcohol and drug problems in the workplace

A. Introduction

Perhaps the single most important factor, to understand the relation alcohol and the workplace in Denmark, is a predominant aspect of Danish culture: It is the dissociation from control and regulation of the members of society and their social groupings. It pervades the daily life and organizational life, and in the last connection discussions of control and regulation have for a longer period dominated the alcohol-work debate. This has been the picture up till the last three to four years at least. Some of the reasons for this development will be discussed below.

I have referred to alcohol in the opening remarks only. The reason being that although drug to some degree presents a general problem in the Danish society, it very seldom - not to say never - has been brought up in relation to work life, maybe except with regard to prescribed drugs. But the responses to the drug issues presented in the project instruments of course will be dealt with below also.

But no cultural artifact - and alcohol and drug regarded as such - can be understood isolated from the broader culture or subculture in which it exists. The remainder of the text will be facts and figures for the context that Denmark sets for the specific area workplace alcohol and drug problems therefore.

The double perspective of alcohol and drug makes it somewhat difficult to give a coherent picture, there have been and to a great extent still are different political views and political reactions in relation to the two kinds of psychoactive substances. In responding to the questionnaire and in the interview situation the participants in the project are asked to evaluate the development through a three year period. But in this section an extension of the period will be used to create a frame of understanding of the present situation.

B. Alcohol Consumption

Entering the century, the per capita alcohol consumption in Denmark was relatively high (a. 13 l. pure alcohol) but with a downward tendency. The distribution over the beverages characterized Denmark as a spirits consuming country with more than two third of the consumed alcohol being spirits and the rest beer, wine covering only a very minor percentage. One major event influenced the consumption level and patterns. Over a year (in 1917) the government raised the excises to such an extent that a bottle of the most common spirit (Danish Aquavit: 40% of alcohol) in the detail sale went up from approximately one Danish krone to ten Danish kroner, a rise of 1000%. An immediate reaction was a fall in the sale (consumption) of spirits, which after some turbulence over a few years levelled at about 25% of the total consumption. The total consumption was reduced by this rise in spirits prices of course (from a. 13 to a. 4 litres pure alcohol per capita), but solely through the spirits while beer and wine, though the prices for these two beverages also were raised (doubled), kept their levels now constituting about 70% (beer) and 5% (wine) of the total comsumption.

The reason that this event has been taken up is, that the change caused in the consumption pattern by the cultural and economical chock - "over-night" changing the prevailing dominance of spirits to a domination of beer - seems to have been unchallenged until the last two decades.

From 1918 until about 1955 the average consumption in Denmark was pendling at a level from about 3 to 4.5 litres pure alcohol[1] (table 3).

---

[1] All figures for the average consumption will be of the population above the age of 14.

Table 3: Average consumption in 100% alcohol per inhabitant over the age of 14.

Year	Litres 100% alcohol
1900	13.0
1910	10.7
1920	4.1
1930	3.6
1940	2.9
1950	4.5
1960	5.4
1970	8.7
1980	11.7
1981	12.1
1982	12.4
1983	12.8
1984	12.2
1985	12.3
1986	12.1
1987	11.9
1988	11.6
1989	11.5
1990	11.6
1991	11.5
1992	11.8

From 1955 to the mid seventies the consumption was nearly tripled (in 1983: 12.8 litres), leading to a levelling out until the mid eighties, from which time the official sales figures have shown a decline of about 10%, the figures for 1990 being 11.6 litres pure alcohol per person over 14 years. During the rise and in the plateau period a change in consumption patterns took place. After the Second World War the spirits consumption went up and in the seventies approached 20% of the total consumption. But for the last six to eight years the spirits consumption has been relatively stable around 14-15%. As can be seen in table 4, the major change has been between beer and wine, the latter taking a steady growing part, and now seems to have established itself at a 25% level, meaning that beer "is down" to around the 60% of the total consumption. For further information see annex two. The results presented in this annex have a direct bearing on the understanding of data from the project.

**Table 4: Distribution of type of beverages consumed (Percentage)
(Source: Danish Statistics).**

Type of alcohol	1960	1970	1980	1990	1993
Beer	74	70	62	60	59
Wine	9	10	18	25	29
Spirits	17	20	20	15	12
Total consumption Litres pure alcohol	5.4	8.7	11.7	11.6	11.8

One factor, which gives problems in estimating the average consumption, is that the prize level in Denmark is rather high and that quite many Danes have fairly easy access to a market in Germany with low prices on alcohol. About 1.5 million Danes live within a two hours drive from the nearest German city (Flensburg) and have until recently been able to buy alcohol of about half the Danish price. From 1992 the price difference has been somewhat reduced; on the other hand, the amount allowed to be brought back home from a one day visit greatly increased. But in 1990 the amount allowed to bring back from a one day visit was 12 litres of beer, 5 litres of wine and 3 litres of fortified wine. This would cost about 70 ECU in Denmark for inexpensive wines and aperitifs and ordinary beers. In Germany the price would be about 34 ECU for identical purchases. The dark figure of unregistered alcohol purchase is expected to be fairly high therefore, and from customs statistics and questionnaires to border traders it is assumed that the official sales figures from the Danish Statistical Bureau for the period in the late eighties should have increased by 12-15% (Thorsen, 1988). A recent investigation indicates, however, that the border trade regarding alcohol has been somewhat reduced. Part of the purchase of especially the cheap beer in Germany has been taken over by a growing sale of discount beer in Denmark. (Milhøj, 1993). It is estimated, though, that the Danish beer consumption figures in 1993 should be about 7% higher due to the border trade.

The Danish Statistical Bureau calculates figures of the percentage alcohol purchases constitutes of the total household expenditure. For the last decade this figure has been fairly stable about 2.5-3.0%. Regarding home production (legal or illegal) of wine, beer or alcohol investigations seem to indicate that it can be regarded as negligible (Rasmussen & Sabroe, 1989).

C.   Danish Alcohol Policy

In 1985, WHO took initiative to a stressing of the importance of development of national alcohol policies (Grant, 1985). Denmark has not taken a prominent position in the discussion of the necessity of an alcohol policy. Some critics of the Danish attitude claim that it is choice of words when the Danish Government argues that Denmark has an alcohol policy and characterizes our alcohol policy as *liberal*. A more accurate description of the policy - if one could say that any such exists - would be *indifference* according to these critics with the implicit understanding that one does not face the alcohol related problems resulting from the high Danish (per capita) consumption. Though a statement like this might get support especially from our Scandinavian brothers and sisters, it is unlikely that the view would be accepted or be understood in its problem-formulation among Danish politicians or the common Danes. Danish alcohol policy has for many years been dominated by the assumption "that ... a liberal attitude, relatively free of restrictions will give the best long term re-sults" (Minister of Social Affairs in the Danish Parliament, March 1984). Backing of this policy runs across party lines in the Danish Parliament and must be considered to have a profound foothold in the population also.

Implementation of general restrictions is contrary to Danish policies thus. The view is that concrete problems ought to be dealt with in relation to the single human being, not through broad sweeping general restrictions or other population based efforts. The view includes an accentuation of a personal responsibility for own life, and not the least personal responsibility in relation to risk situations. Culturally speaking, *control* is not a concept that goes down well with Danes, and not only because it suggests curtailment of personal freedoms. There seems to be a firm belief also that *more restrictions* and *ex-panded control not* will cause a reduction in consumption, rather on the contrary, bringing the "*prohibited*" into focus can lead to the opposite effect. Another fundamental supposition in relation to the conducted policy is that a grown-up person, generally, will be able to or ought to be able to make his/her own (responsible) choices, concerning consumption of alcohol *also*. But it is important at the same time that a necessary foundation for choosing is present; establishing a high level of information and knowledge therefore is a central aspect of Danish alcohol policy, and constitutes the principal elements of the contributions towards alcohol related problems in Denmark together with the legalized treatment-efforts. "Restrictive" points of view only manifest themselves in the very high level of taxation for alcohol, especially for spirits. Thus the classical threefold: *control, restricted availability* and *price setting* is in the main only utilised with regard to the last mentioned in Denmark.

23

It is obvious that it is the *use* more than the *abuse*, which has been the take-off for Danish alcohol policy, a policy which many critics would say in reality is non-existent because it intervenes to such a minimal extent and only slightly takes a position on abuse and alcohol related problems. But there is no doubt that a great majority of the Danish Parliament finds, an alcohol policy exists, which as previously indicated comprises *high level of alcohol taxation*, stress on *individual responsibility, information, knowledge, preventive efforts* and a *high degree of readiness in the health system* if the individual should develop a misuse. It is assumed also and more or less stated explicitly during negotiations and in governmental orders, that the conducted alcohol policy in general will dedramatize the situation regarding alcohol and a criminalization of the alcohol area supposedly does not come into being. The prevailing attitudes ensure that the abuser is not stigmatized and the conditions for a treatment effort and a restoration of the individual in society is optimal therefore. But again critics raise their voices and claim that the other side of the picture is the risk, that the subject of alcohol abuse becomes tabooed, and that the individual in the name of liberality and non-involvement too late is confronted with the consequences of his/her heavy consumption of alcohol. The newest statement of Danish alcohol policy appears in the November 1992 edition of "Nordic Alcohol journal", in which the then Danish minister of Health states: " ... That alcohol is part of everyday life in Denmark and of Danish Culture... (the) task is to prevent the level of consumption resulting in damages... (we are) not interested in guardianship, in restrictions and prohibitions. The core element in Danish alcohol policy is an attempt to have the individual taking responsibility for his own consumption (of alcohol)" (NAT, 1992, p. 280).

The most recent general statement relating to the workplace is given in a publication of November 1991 issued by the Ministry of Health on behalf of several ministries: Industry, Justice, Taxation, Social Affairs and Education. In a section named "Alcohol policy and the workplace" it is stated: "The Government sees it as an essential task in general to change the attitude regarding alcohol misuse. A conscious alcohol policy in the workplace plays an important role in this connection. Openess about alcohol problems in the workplace has not only an immediate and local effect but can in general be part of a preventive effort by breaking down taboos regarding alcohol misuse.

The understanding of the importance in dealing with eventual alcohol problems is growing. In this connection it is positive that both the employers' and workers' organizations support this new openess and take part in the actual debate.

Understanding and openess are important preconditions to be able to set in an early effort in dealing with an alcohol abuse and enhance the possibility to interfere before damage takes place.

The Goverment agrees with the organization's view that the discussion of how an alcohol policy should be approached has to be carried out in the single enterprise. The problem should be dealt with as part of the general local personnel policy." (Sundhedsministeriet, 1991).

Not withstanding these political considerations an important message can be taken from Sabroe (1991, 1994, Sabroe & Laursen, 1994). In surveys asking representative populations about their attitudes towards alcohol and work, a growing percentage supports a prohibition of alcohol in the workplace. In 1989 the figure was 41% supporting a prohibition (the question being: Free availability, restricted availability or prohibition). In 1990 and 1994 the figure rose to 70% the question being different, however: A four-scale of strongly agree to strongly disagree on the statement that Danish workplaces ought to have an alcohol prohibition. The 70% represent answers of strongly agree/agree, (see also p. 29 ff).

D.   Alcohol Related Problems

In an analysis of consumption and alcohol related problems (Thorsen, 1990) it has been shown that most alcohol related diagnoses have had a rise during the seventies and eighties and a rather strong correlation is found between level of total consumption and registered deaths from alcohol psychosis, alcoholism, alcohol poisoning and delirium tremens. The correlation has been somewhat "off the line" in the later years, however. In spite of a fall in average consumption of more than 10% since the mid-eighties, the growth is continuing in the registered alcohol related problems, especially chirrosis (Sundhedsstyrelsen, 1991, 1992). Also for alcohol related problems as drunken driving, arrests for drunken behaviour and criminal offences under the influence of alcohol a rise can be shown. But a stagnation seems to appear in the late eighties going towards a decline in 1990-91.

The rise in average consumption during the sixties and seventies can be a-scribed to an increased consumption of wine clearly. Consumption of beer and spirits dropped during the period. Supposedly a major population oriented factor is that women have increased their consumption especially from the middle and upper social strata (Sabroe, 1991) and women are in the ascent also with regard to the share of registered alcohol related problems having rises from 30 to 50 percent during the last 10-15 years. Regarding treatment at alcohol ambulatories the rise in the given period was 20% for men and 65% for women. The most recent figures (1987) for alcohol related problems - *all in number per 100,000 aged 15 years and above* - are given below (Sundhedsstyrelsen 1991, 1992). The tendency comments are based on Danish Statistics from 1993 and 1994 (Danmarks Statistik 1994, Politiets årsberetning 1993).

1. *Alcohol psychosis (including D.T.), alcoholism and alcohol poisoning.* Death rate: 4.3; discharges from hospitals: 257.4 for men, 91.1 for women. The figures have been increasing during the last 10 years. In 1991 a decline appeared, however.

2. *Liver cirrhosis.* Death rate: 16.7. Discharges from hospitals: 84.7 for men and 58.2 for women. These figures have been relatively stable during the last 10 years.

3. *Pancreatitis.* Death rate: 2.0; discharges from hospitals: 103.6 for men, 42.5 for women. Within the last 10 years relatively stable figures.

4. *Hospitalization with main diagnosis alcoholism:* 40.8 (equals to 16.4% of all categories of diagnoses). The figures have been increasing the last 10 years.

5. *Alcohol related traffic accidents.* Alcohol related deaths: 32% of all traffic deaths. Alcohol related accidents: 19.3% of all traffic accidents. Charges for drunken driving about 20.000 annually. Figures declining in the later years.

6. *Arrests for drunken behaviour:* The police figures are given in rates of per 1000 inhabitants and have, after a peak into the early eighties, been relatively stable at a rate of 3.4 for the last two decades.

Supplementary to these figures the Danish Health Council has calculated (Sundhedsstyrelsen, 1991):

7. 4% of all *deaths* in 1989 had an alcohol related diagnosis as first, secondary or tertiary diagnosis.

8. 24% of all *psychiatric patients* had an alcohol related main or subdiagnosis.

In the same source, the Danish Health Council also made an evaluation over the development in certain alcohol related problems in the five year period of 1985-89. The results showed a complicated pattern (ibid.):

1. The average alcohol consumption declined 5%. In the early nineties a rise of the same size has appeared.

2. Alcohol related traffic accidents *declined* 18%. This tendency continued in the early nineties.

3. The percentage of alcohol related traffic deaths *declined* 12%. The figure has been stable in the early nineties.

4. The percentage charged with alcohol driving *rose* with 7%. In the early nineties a decline of 25% has taken place.

5. Death recorded as alcohol related *rose* with 15%.

6. Discharges from somatic hospitals with an alcohol related diagnosis *rose* with 19%.

Thorsen (1990) and Sundhedsstyrelsen (1991) are strong adherents to the assumption that these figures are determined to a high degree by the relatively high average consumption in Denmark, thus being in favour of the disputed "total consumption model" of alcohol related problems. For further and detailed information on the data see *annex five*.

Accidents at work - alcohol related?

According to Danish Emergency Ward statistics (Nøgletal, 1992), 3% of all hospitalized after accidents can be characterized as work-related. This figure has been declining over the last five years, in 1987 being 4.5%. Figures from emergency ward statistics also indicate that only a very minor part of these are assigned to alcohol (or drug) influence. It has been argued that maybe a greater dark-figure exists on account of a tendency not to report an accident if alcohol had been involved unless treatment is of absolute necessity. This has *not* been supported by systematically collected data, however.

E.   Danish Drug Policy

Drug didn't appear as an issue in the public debate until the late 1960es, although an Act of Euphoriant Substances was passed in the Danish parliament in 1955 already. This law criminalized import and export, selling, buying, distributing, receiving, producing and possessing a long series of euphorizing substances. In itself, drug use is not a criminal offence according to Danish legislation, but implicitly it is covered by the criminal status applied to drug acquisition. Nor is possession of drugs by a user a specific offence unless it is in connection with trafficking (Leroy, 1991). In 1969 the general Penal Law was supplemented with a paragraph (section 191) oriented towards professional drug crime, the maximum penalties being six years. In 1975 the maximum penalties under this section were raised to ten years.

In the beginning the drug use was fairly isolated with the hippie movement and the youth revolution having a user group of young and relatively well educated thus. But rather quick a spread took place involving especially youngsters from the lower social strata. From the start the main pattern was a mixed abuse including alcohol, narcotics and medicine. It is an interesting fact that heroin does not appear really in the Danish drug market until early 1978, from which time it became the main drug for intravenous use. From the mid eighties amphetamines reappeared after having been very low for quite many years. Cocaine has not been established as a common drug at the street level in Denmark until the present.

Throughout the seventies and eighties there was a steady trend towards an abuser population more and more socially tainted, and at the same time drug abuse was characterized by the professional organization of the trade to a still higher degree. In preventive and treatment efforts a generally accepted view by politicians and therapists was "... that drug abuse could not be explained as an illness, but had to be regarded as a complicated individual reaction, predominantly, caused by straining and imperfect conditions of life" (Folketingsforhandlinger (Parliament debate), 1979).

Two major debates on drugs have been accomplished in the Danish parliament only, one being in 1979 and another in 1984. The first debate was oriented towards a better registration of the dimensions of the drug problems, to control the supply of drugs and how to improve prevention and treatment. In the second the question of methadone in treatment of drug abuse was central. Methadone is now officially used in treatment of narcotics in Denmark.

Results from a survey carried out by the National Health Authorities give a picture of the Danish drug (table 5). The main result is that cannabis is the only drug with a major distribution in the population. For other drugs the incidence is small (1-3%). There is no indication - based on several surveys - that the debut age for trying cannabis has become lower, but it is obvious that use of cannabis

Table 5: Drug experimentation and use (above the age of 16)
(Source: Sundhedsstyrelsen, 1991)

	Cannabis	Amphetamines	Cocaine	Heroine
Ever tried	21.1%	3.0%	1.1%	0.1%
Tried within the last year	4.6%	0.7%	0.2%	0.06%
N=1534				

is a young age phenomenon. 17% of the 16-19 year-old state that they have tried cannabis within the last year. For the 40-45 year-old the figure is 1%. In the younger years the gender distribution among users is about equal, but in the later age groups one third more men are users than women (ibid.). It seems that a mixed abuse has increased among especially young people with social or phychic problems, mostly being a cannabis-alcohol combination but also including amphetamines. Another tendency causing some alarm is that smoking heroine has appeared among youngsters. Presumably they are under the impression that the risk of addiction is greatly reduced/not present smoking the heroine.

Figures from seizures of drugs in the country and from charges of drug-related crime could give supplementary information of the size of the problem, although some of the seizures, particularly cocaine at Kastrup Airport, suggest that it has been in transit mainly. The tendency for the latter part of the 1980s has been an increase in the supply of all drugs with cannabis clearly taking the biggest share, and amphetamine reappearing (ref. table 1 in *appendix two*). A rise has definitely taken place since the mid-eighties, but there is considerably fluctuations in the respective amount seizured. In 1989 the cocaine figures were very high and in 1992 the amphetamine figures. It should be noted also that prescription of methadone to addicts, who are difficult to reach from the treatment system, was greatly increased. An increasing concern bears on the amount of methadone getting into the drug market. From the mid-eighties to 1992 the methadone seizured rose from approx. 1,300 ml. and 600 tablets to 17,416 ml./4527 tablets.

Charges of drug related crime also increased, the greatest rise for the less serious crimes (possession for own use and small amount sale to finance own use) being more than sixty percent over the last five years of the eighties (table 2, *appendix two*).

Other figures to supplement the picture are 1) That the excess mortality rate for drug abusers is 20 times the normal rate for the age group, and that this figure seems stable. At all 208 deaths were registered in 1992 chiefly with poisoning as cause. 2) The gender distribution is 2/3 men and 1/3 women. 3) The average age - especially among heroin addicts and methadone "substitution-treated" - has grown. For further information see *annex four*.

During the later years of the eighties and first years of the nineties the AIDS incidense rose from approx. 130 (1986) to approx. 1,100 (1992). In the same period the amount of drug-addicts with AIDS also grew, in 1992 being 72 cases (comparing to 6.4% of all AIDS cases).

F.   Research on Alcohol and Drugs in the Workplace

In annex two data are presented which provide us with a general frame of understanding giving a profile of the quantitative distribution of the alcohol consumption in Denmark, according to time of day, day of week, gender, age and type of alcohol. The results tell us that only a very minor part of Danish alcohol consumption takes place at the workplace. As a general frame, these data are necessary information to understand the results obtained in the present report.

As an issue in research the relation alcohol and the workplace has been insufficiently dealt with. This is partly a picture of the general situation of alcohol research in Denmark, which until the last couple of years has had a very low priority, and the researchers having established the frail beginning of an alcohol research milieu still have to fight for their existence. The other reason for the absence partly might be the until recently obvious taboo-character of the topic, partly due to a general attitude of non-interference (being a person's "own decision") at the individual level and partly due to the potential conflict character of the subject in the worker-employer relationship. But research results do exist. Above was mentioned the figures from Hansen & Andersen (1989). Another and major research is undertaken by Colling (1989), who in an investigation from The National Social Research Institute sent a questionnaire to 4000 Danish enterprises and followed up by qualitative interviews and observational studies at selected workplaces. Most of the questionnaires were answered by the management, and a general response was that alcohol was not a major problem at the workplaces. The qualitative part of the investigation aimed at seeing relations between alcohol consumption patterns and the conditions of work or enterprise culture. As a consequence of this research Colling (ibid., 1991) argues that to improve the situation more culture sensitive prevention strategies must be developed. It is not enough to establish a policy that seeks to establish certain formalized norms regarding individual alcohol behaviour at the workplace. One has to include the complicated pattern of work structure, work processes, traditions, organizational hierarchies, relations with the surroundings etc., all of which do have an impact on the alcohol culture of the workplace.

In another survey of 2000 representative Danes (above the age of fifteen), six out of 62 questions were related to alcohol and work (Sabroe, 1994). In summing up on this it is stated (ibid. p. 107) "... that the results do not seem to indicate that alcohol is a major problem at Danish workplaces, and not at all at a level regarding consumed alcohol and work problems related to it voiced by the Danish media in the later years." This result is in accordance with other research as mentioned above. The results further indicate that only *just under four out of every hundred daily consume alcohol at work* and the amount for the majority of these are restricted to from one to a few beers. But the *men* - as it is a fact for the common consumption - carry the main responsibility for the consumption with more than *seven out of every hundred*. It is particularly the twenty to fifty ear old men who take alcohol at work, and with regard to occupation the skilled workers and independents top the list with respectively ten and six out of every hundred, who daily have alcohol at work. The question if alcohol should be in workplaces at all divides the population in such a way that *a little majority is in favour of access to alcohol*. But *less than nine out of every hundred are of the opinion that access should be free*, while just over two fifths of the population find that access should be limited, and two out of five go in for prohibition. It is (again) the skilled workers and employees/civil servants who support free or limited access to the highest degree.

In a recent investigation (Sabroe, 1991) the question of prohibition of alcohol at the workplace was also raised. A further movement towards a prohibition attitude seems to have taken place. In table 6 the figures prove that a majority of 70.1% strongly agree or agree in prohibition of alcohol at the workplace.

**Table 6: Attitude to prohibition of alcohol at the workplace
and average level of own consumption**

Attitude to prohibition	Percentage	Units per week
Strongly agree in prohibition	46.6	5.74
Mostly agree in prohibition	23.5	7.92
Mostly disagree in prohibition	14.1	8.68
Strongly disagree in prohibition	12.3	11.10
(No answer)	3.5	-

The table also points at a strong relation between own consumption and attitude. The bigger the amount of alcohol drunk per week the more one disagrees in prohibition. These figures are supported by data from a 1994 (representative) survey in which also 70% strongly agreed or agreed in prohibition of alcohol in the workplace (Sabroe & Laursen, 1994).

Half the population has worked together with a person during her/his worklife, who had a high alcohol consumption. It is a big figure which could seem to be in contradiction to the above mentioned figures, but supposedly the figure reflects the wording of the question and that it is a question of lifetime information. In about half of the reported cases interventions have been undertaken, primarily from management but also to some extent from work colleagues and relatively seldom from shop stewards (Sabroe, 1994).

The tables documenting these results are shown in *annex three*.

Seeing in the perspective of the research results from Danish research on alcohol and work life from the last five to seven years, the overall picture is of a great overlap in results: Alcohol seems *not* to be experienced as a problem at the great majority of the Danish workplaces, though the results have been obtained with different methodology and therefore can be difficult to compare (Nielsen, 1982; Sælan, 1984; Hansen & Andersen, 1985; Aarhus Amtskommune, 1988; Colling, 1989; Sabroe, 1994). But apart from this ascertainment it seems that there is a continuation of the tendency suggested by Hansen & Andersen (1985) that the Danish consumption pattern is changing from previous having had an essential day-consumption in the workplace to a predominant consumption during the evenings and especially during the weekends.

The results from the representative population can have an interest, not the least because the last few years have witnessed a debate in the media, founded on myths and suppositions than real information. The debate has singled out alcohol as a considerable problem for the labour market and claimed that solutions were difficult because of the attitudes (especially among employees) in relation to a regulation (often expressed as prohibition) of access to alcohol in the workplace. From the investigation a picture can be drawn now, indicating that the debate has been somewhat distorted, at least with regard to the consumption. Assertions to the effect that one third of the total Danish alcohol consumption is related to the workplace (Sælan, 1985) thus seem to be far off. It will be essential to remember henceforth, that irrespective of the fact that alcohol prohibition is not a predominant situation in Danish workplaces it is a little minority (the daily users which amounts to scarcely 4%) for whom alcohol at work *could* be a problem eventually. The hypothetical form and the word problem (instead of abuse) is used by purpose. There is nothing in the results which indicates the extent of the daily consumption, an estimation based on supplementary figures indicates that for the great majority the amount is very small, however. But looking at the question of regulating alcohol in the workplace an important message to the decision-takers is that *by far the main part (more than 7 out of every 10) is prepared for a prohibition of alcohol in the workplace.*

Irrespective of the dimension of the problem, a pattern clearly emerge of a workplace consumption which reflects the common consumption patterns in society. The universal socio-economic relations rather than the characteristics of the workplace seem to determine the consumption, even though it is possible to draw a consistent picture in relation to the consumption of the different groups of occupation. The pattern of consumption indicates that a preventive effort should be aimed at the leisure sector, but that workplaces could be an important media for this effort.

No research has been found in the available literature dealing with drugs in the Danish workplace.

G.   Frequency of Alcohol and Drug Related Problems

Seen across employers' organizations, employees' organizations as well as enterprises, a similar pattern appears in the views on problems experienced in the workplace. For alcohol the dominant reaction is in ten of the thirteen questions that they "sometimes" had been experienced amongst the members (tables 7 and 8). For three items: Employee-supervisor conflict, damage to property and theft the dominant reaction was a "never". These views were substantiated in the interviews, but it is necessary to remind of the comment given by a majority of the interviewees and already mentioned page 14. They found the response scale difficult to use, arguing that "never" was a too ultimate (zero) category and "sometimes" was experienced as indicating too much in relation to what one wished to express! "Sometimes" thus for most respondents was used as expressing "seldom" if not "seldom, if ever".

For drugs the pattern also were consistent across the participants though it in interviews were expressed that the questionnaire markings were given with great faltering because so little was known about the field and in general illegal drugs were thought of as a "non-existing" problem. However, concern was stated in the interviews for prescribed drugs on the grounds that one knew of a high consumption of prescribed analgetica, anxiolytica and hypnotica in general.

For drugs, the dominant pattern were "unknown" (and no answer) followed by "never" for organizations. Two organizations (employee-) indicated that drugs "sometimes" could cause a series of problems, however, (table 7). Enterprises had similar patterns in their response (table 8).

As previously indicated the consensus is high regarding the attitude that drugs (with the exception of prescribed medicine) do not present a problem for the Danish workplace and is not given special attention in enterprise policies.

Table 7: Frequency of alcohol and drug-related work problems encountered during the past three years (organizations' response)

Work problem	Alcohol related				Drug related				Missing	
	Never	Sometimes	Often	Unknown	Never	Sometimes	Often	Unknown	A	D
Absence from work		5		1	2	1		3	3	3
Employee Supervisor conflict	2	3	1	1	4	1		3	3	3
Accidents or injuries at work	1	5		1	4	1		3	2	3
Safety violations	1	5	1	1	4	1		3	2	2
Impaired performance		3	2	2	2	2		3	2	3
Reduced motivation		5	1	2	2	2		3	2	3
Disciplinary problems	1	3	1	2	2	2		3	3	3
Lateness		4	1	2	2	2		3	3	3
Intoxication at work	1	4		2	2	2		3	3	3
Conflict with work colleagues	1	5		1	2	2		3	3	3
Damage to equipment/ property	2	2		3	2	2		3	3	3
Dismissals/terminations		5		1	2	2		3	4	3
Theft of company property	1	4		2	2	2		3	3	3

Table 8: Frequency of alcohol and drug related work problems, encountered during the past three years (enterprises response)

Work problem	Alcohol related				Drug related				Missing	
	Never	Sometimes	Often	Unknown	Never	Sometimes	Often	Unknown	A	D
Absence from work		6			2	2		1	1	2
Employee Supervisor conflict	4	2			3	2			1	2
Accidents or injuries at work		6			3	1		1	1	2
Safety violations		6			3	1		1	1	2
Impaired performance		6			2	2		1	1	2
Reduced motivation		6			3	1		1	1	2
Disciplinary problems	1	5			2	1		1	1	2
Lateness		6			2	2		1	1	2
Intoxication at work	1	6			2	2		1		2
Conflict with work colleagues	2	4			3	1		1	1	2
Damage to equipment/ property	5	1			4			1	1	2
Dismissals/terminations	1	6			2	2		1		2
Theft of company property	5	1			3	1		1	1	2

Most participants expressed a concern of alcohol as a possible cause for work-related problems in the workplace (table 9). At the same time the majority is of the opinion that the number of employees with alcohol related problems are decreasing, only two (employee) organizations being of the view that they are increasing.

The uncertainty of how to respond to the questions raised about drugs and the possible underlying problems is mirrored in the figures from the questions on level of concern and development in problems. Reflecting on concern about drugs as a possible cause for workplace problems the participants display a divided picture. The predominant pattern is "not concerned at all" for cocaine/stimulants and opiates, whereas the response are "somewhat concerned" regarding cannabis and prescribed drugs, the organizations being slightly more concerned than the enterprises (table 9). The predominant reaction to questions of increasing or decreasing of drug problems of members is an "unsure", an exception being three organizations which state a decreasing for cannabis and increasing for prescribed drugs, and one enterprise takes the latter view also (table 10).

Table 9: Level of concern regarding alcohol and drug use as potential causes of work-related problems

Substance	Enterprises				Organizations				
	Not concerned at all	Somewhat concerned	Very concerned	Unsure	Not concerned at all	Somewhat concerned	Very concerned	Unsure	Missing
Alcohol	2	3	2		1	8	1		1
Cannabis	3	2	1	1	4	5			1
Cocaine/stimulants	4	1		2	5	2	2		1
Opiates	4	1		2	5	2		2	1
Prescribed drugs	3	2	2		1	6	1	1	1

Table 10: Increase/decrease in problems with alcohol or drugs

Substance	Enterprises			Organizations			
	Increasing	Decreasing	Unsure	Increasing	Decreasing	Unsure	Missing
Alcohol		3	4	2	5	2	1
Cannabis	1		6		3	6	1
Cocaine/stimulants			7			9	1
Opiates			7			9	1
Prescribed drugs	1		6	2	1	6	1

H. Attitudes towards the Nature of the Problem

In both the enterprise and the organization questionnaire a question with five statements concerning attitudes towards alcohol and drug problems was presented. The five statements were:

Our organization ...

1. ... seems to have more members with alcohol or drug problems than other industries
2. ... has the kind of work where efficiency and safety could be seriously affected by alcohol or drug use
3. ... has placed a high priority on the prevention of problem alcohol or drug use affecting the workplace
4. ... considers that work-related problems arising from problem alcohol or drug use are causing significant costs
5. ... has work demands and stress levels which may contribute to the development of alcohol and drug related problems

The responses are shown in table 11.

Table 11: Attitudes towards the nature of alcohol and drug problems

Statement no.	Enterprises					Organizations				
	Strongly agree	Agree	Disagree	Strongly disagree	Unsure	Strongly agree	Agree	Disagree	Strongly disagree	Unsure
1			1	6				4	6	
2	4	3				5	5			
3	4	3				2	4	4		
4	5	2				5	3	1		
5		3	2	2		2	4	2		2

It is obvious that no enterprise neither any organization wish to see themselves as worse off than others. On the other hand they agree that their enterprises/organizations have working conditions that could be seriously affected by alcohol - and drug problems. The table proves a certain similarity in responses from enterprises and organizations, though. In statement 3 and 5 one finds responses that could be related to the traditional division of the labour market, however.

III. Policy and organizational aspects

A. General Background

One cannot say that Denmark has an alcohol policy elaborated in a body of laws. But a law of administration exists of social and health oriented matters, and under this law the responsibility for prevention and treatment of alcohol and drug abuse have - through a series of regulations - been given to the local level (counties and municipalities). The regulations demand that the counties for three year periods develop a theme-plan indicating which areas the county wishes to pay special attention besides the daily routine efforts. Supplementary to this local contribution, the state level participates in treatment efforts through wards at somatic and psychiatric hospitals. Major prevention campaigns are run by the Danish Health Council (Ministry of Health) also.

The role of the state is expected to be maintaining a general preventive effort, continuously to bring into attention the possible dangers of an over-consumption and in general to inspire to a sensible relation to alcohol, as the then Danish Minister of Health expressed it in November 1992 (see page 23).

In the concrete, the state during the last three years has intensified the efforts and launched one major alcohol prevention campaign each year (usually in week 40). The campaign has used a broad spectrum of media presentations and presented a special prevention-theme. These themes have been "the 40-years old and their drinking", "women and drinking", "count your drinks" and "alcohol as a potential life activity diminisher". Written materials have been issued related to the campaigns, among them a "subject-sheet" dealing with alcohol and work (see *annex seven*). In the last national campaign (1994) a paper has been issued in which alcohol and work is an essential part, and in the county follow up on the campaign the workplace has been an important target of the information efforts.

In all counties and in the municipalities exists a social and health department. In the counties this includes a special consultative body for alcohol and drug prevention and treatment. In several of the counties has been established a close co-operation between the alcohol and drug consultants and the labour market. Joint preventive efforts have been undertaken, and one county has made a workplace kit similar to the one constructed by ILO. In some counties one find a close co-operation between the major enterprises having an alcohol policy and the county consultants regarding assistance to employees with alcohol problems.

At the local level the counties autonomously decide the priority of the different areas of the problem field including the share of preventive work as against treatment. But the former, in the later years, has gained in interest and generally the view is, that a preventive effort should give general knowledge and information. Giving an informative education in the school, establishing the best possible condition for children and young to develop their cognitive and physical abilities, providing them with a safe and challenging surrounding the best results are considered to be achieved. It is obligatory that the topic of alcohol and drug is taken into the curricula of school children in the 7th to 9th grade. The prevention method primarily used for alcohol as well as drug is providing knowledge and information, to the school children and youngsters. Central in the method is that all children and youngsters should be given the prerequisites to have a proper relation to alcohol, meaning knowledge and attitudes which enables them to deal with alcohol as part of Danish culture and daily life. In relation to drugs the aim is to prevent any contact with the substances. In this connection the entire attitude still is one of re-striction/prohibition and control, being the case not only for "heavy" drugs but also for cannabis. In the last couple of years greater emphasis has been placed on bringing in the parents as a target group for information, creating a basis for mutual informed communication in the family thus.

B.   Alcohol, Drug and the Workplace

Until the last decade the question of alcohol was rather seldom discussed in labour market relations. The existance of alcohol-related problems was acknowledged, though, but it was almost a taboo-subject in discussions, and no initiatives were taken. In the second half of the eighties the question started to appear in the media, even that a follow-up survey (Hansen & Andersen, 1985) stated that in the period from 1975 to 1985 a considerable reduction of drinking in the workplace seemed to have happened. It was clearly not through a general reduction of the average consumption, on the contrary, the consumption increased. But a change to a pattern of home-life drinking occured through the period. Some negotiations took place, also, but in the beginning with little success as the topic was placed in the context of a "traditional" worker-employer clash. In the last three to four years some new trends have appeared in two ways. First at the level of the single enterprise the subject of establishing an alcohol policy has been taken up in the local joint industrial councils, this especially being the case in some of the major workplaces. In fact, these nego-tiations have often resulted in a formal alcohol policy. Second approaches as previously mentioned have been taken at the organizational level, the first resulting in a publication from the Danish Employers' Confederation (Grunnet, 1990) being followed by a jointly issued report from the employers' and workers' main organizations on "Alcohol and employee development" (Grunnet & Bang, 1991). The most recent initiative has been taken by the Main Joint Industrial Council, in which an agreement has been reached of making a pamphlet for general distribution being about "recommendations for an alcohol policy in the workplace" (DA/LO, 1992), see p. 55. Funded by the State Health Council, and produced for the counties in Denmark, a video has been made dealing with the price some employees have to pay as a consequence of a missing alcohol policy. The video is freely distributed to enterprises.

In a recent investigation undertaken by the Confederation of Employers, the 1200 enterprises being of a size that according to legislation demands establishing a joint industrial council were asked, if they had a formulated alcohol policy. The results indicate that a marked progress has taken place in the three year period since 1989, at which time the bigger enterprises with an elaborated personnel policy had or considered to have alcohol policy as an integral part. Today it is estimated that 80% of all enterprises with a joint industrial council have established an alcohol policy, five per cent are having considerations while fifteen per cent have no plans of taking up an alcohol policy. The change in attitude has had the result that 65% of smaller enterprises (less than 50 employees) and 80% of medium size enterprises (50-100 employees) have an alcohol policy. For the bigger enterprises (more than 100 employees) the figure is 90% (DA, 1992). It should be said, however, that these figures are generalized from an investigation having a relatively low response-rate.

This recent activity from the enterprises and organizations might be the reason that the government seems reluctant to take an initiative. The following quotation from the then Danish Minister of Health, Mrs. Esther Larsen, illustrates this: "The enterprises in the 1990'ies will to a higher degree stake on healthy employees. These are creative, they have a surplus to tackle problems and have very few sick-days ... about alcohol policy for the enterprises there is a quite good development at present. The parties of the labour market have in a good way taken a hold of the problem themselves. *In fact so good, that it is my opinion that politicians should not interfere*" (Larsen, 1991). This point of view seems to be supported by a majority of the Danish parliament, at least no special indication of an initiative towards the labour market has been presented in the political negotiations (in the Autumn 1992) on creating funds for a preventive and an extended research effort in relation to alcohol related problems. The question of drugs has been totally absent from this debate named

41

"the alcohol package", though some attempts have been taken to broaden the subject by talking about substance prevention and research instead of alcohol prevention and research.

C.   Views and Attitudes from enterprises and organizations

In section three of the questionnaire and in the interview, a series of questions was raised on the state of affairs regarding introduction of alcohol policies and their implementation and on the recommended response to employee with alcohol or/and drug problems. The response pattern is shown in table 12.

Table 12: Response to employees with alcohol or other drug problems

Approach	Enterprises			Organizations		
	Alcohol	Illegal drugs	Prescribed drugs	Alcohol	Illegal drugs	Prescribed drugs
Use of health/welfare procedures	2	2	1	5	3	4
Use of disciplinary procedures	3	2	2	2	1	1
Case by case approach based on individual circumstances	4	5	6	8	6	6

The dominant response is a case by case approach based on individual circumstances. From the interviews it became evident that the three possibilities given for response were not experienced as exclusive but as mutually dependent and that health/welfare or disciplinary approaches is to be regarded as following up the case by case approach. Merely one participant (enterprise) stated that a disciplinary procedure should be the only and immediate response.

When policies are established in enterprises they include both alcohol and drugs generally. For the two organizations stating to have a written policy, alcohol is the topic alone. Only one of the seven enterprises has had an alcohol policy in more than ten years (table 13). As already stated above the movement towards establishing written alcohol/drug policies is a fairly recent one. About half of the participating organizations have considerations of the need for an alcohol and drug policy in the workplace.

Table 13: Time of introduction of policies

Policy (Enterprises)	Less than 12 months ago	1-2 years	3-5 years	6-10 years	11 years or more
Alcohol		2		2	1
Drugs		1			
Combined alcohol/drugs		3	1	2	

Policy (Organizations)	Less than 12 months ago	1-2 years	3-5 years	6-10 years	11 years or more
Alcohol	1	1			
Drugs					
Combined alcohol/drugs					

The rules of the policies allow consumption of alcohol under certain restrictions (often indicated as a beer with the lunch) in most enterprises. Generally, the rules include management as well as employees, but with specific exceptions for entertainment of guests or special events in the enterprise life. It seems, from unsystematic information, though, (daily papers etc.), that there is a tendency at the moment to take the full step towards a prohibition introducing alcohol policies. In a clear majority of the cases the developing of an alcohol/drug policy is carried out with extensive consultations between management and employee representative/union. Implementing the policy most enterprises have distributed it to all staff. Answers are missing regarding questions of health promotion courses, formal supervisor training courses and special health staff training courses. No enterprise has answered these questions, the interviews indicating that the problems of alcohol and drugs were not considered major ones. The sole introduction of an alcohol policy was considered sufficient to create a condition ensuring that the marginal number with problems would be "taken care of".

D.   Attitudes towards treatment of alcohol and drug problems

In responding to statements on treatment of alcohol and drug problems one sees a broad agreement again between enterprises and organizations (table 14). In general one could say that a positive attitude is present in the data and this was supported from the interviews. One exception appears, though. More of the enterprises are not particularly optimistic regarding the employees chances to recover and work effectively after having had alcohol or drug problems. This seems to be somewhat in contrast with a support of the statement, that one expects employees to respond well to management or treatment of alcohol/drug problems. Maybe the negation in the statement has brought confusion in responding.

Table 14: Attitudes towards treatment

Item	Enterprises					Organizations				
	Strongly agree	Agree	Disagree	Strongly disagree	Unsure	Strongly agree	Agree	Disagree	Strongly disagree	Unsure
Our organization believes:										
... that employees who develop alcohol or drug related problems respond well to management and/or treatment	3	3			1		6	2		2
... that we do not need to provide assistance or services ourselves because such resources are available from the State	2		4	1			3	2	5	
... that employees who develop alcohol or drug problems are usually unable to recover and work effectively	1	3	3				2	6	2	
... that we have a responsibility to support an employee's treatment and pay any necessary costs	2	3	1	1		4	5	1		

IV. Worker - employer relations

As stated in section I, Denmark is a strongly organized country, and all relationships between employer and employees are laid down in laws and labour market agreements. From the early eighties and until today a situation of "peace" have characterized the labour market. Absence of open traditional conflicts between employer and employees might have been one reason that welfare and working condition matters have been accentuated in the debates in the Main Joint Industrial Council and at the local and enterprise level of joint industrial councils. Alcohol as a workplace problem has been taken up by many enterprises from 1989 especially, when a break through seems to have taken place which to a major extent removed the alcohol problems from a place among the traditional employer-employee conflictual themes. The result has been that a great majority of Danish workplaces with joint industrial councils have an alcohol policy or are considering having one (DA,1992).

It is a characteristic that this trend has originated from the enterprise level and not from the organizational level. It should be said, however, that the Danish Employers Confederation was early in the picture (Grunnet, 1991) and that the Danish Confederation of Trade Unions joined this initiative shortly after. But apart from some very preliminary steps, the topic of alcohol problems has not been dealt with at the branch or regional organization level. And the national organizations themselves had not, at the time of the investigation, been considering an alcohol policy in their offices, neither at central (national) nor at local level.

When establishing the actual policy the main theme is clearly alcohol problems at enterprise level. Drugs (illegal and prescribed) are taken up but to a small extent. Some enterprises include a tobacco policy also, according to an investigation about one third, and a still minor part has taken AIDS into the "policy packet" lately (DA, 1992).

It is the view at organizational level and supported by the enterprises that the negotiations between employer and employees regarding an alcohol/drug policy are kept in a spirit of co-operation generally and that the results are readily accepted by the work force. In the majority of the cases the policy is one of regulations normally allowing a beer during lunch breaks. One enterprise participating and one participating in the project with a few very general comments stated prohibition. A prohibitive alcohol policy seems from these and other information mostly to be present in enterprises dealing with dangerous products or with dangerous production processes.

The result of the co-operation in the Main Joint Industrial Council, mentioned in section III, could be taken as an indicator of the level of understanding arrived at regarding alcohol and drug problems in the workplace. It is important to mention, however, that the outset for this understanding is an underlying agreement that drugs are not considered to be any problem and that alcohol is not a serious problem in Danish workplaces (cf. also annex two and three). Further, the acceptance of the necessity for an alcohol policy is built on a prevention-thinking and as a solidarity with the minority of employees who for many reasons have acquired inappropriate relations to alcohol.

When responding to statements on the relations between management and employee regarding alcohol and drug issues, a homogeneous picture is displayed. With one exception both enterprises and organizations strongly agree or agree that discussions between management and unions on alcohol or drug problems result in broad agreement usually. The same tendency is demonstrated in the supplementary questions shown in table 15.

Table 15: Views on reactions to alcohol and drug problems

Item	Enterprises					Organizations				
	Strongly agree	Agree	Disagree	Strongly disagree	Unsure	Strongly agree	Agree	Disagree	Strongly disagree	Disagree
Our organization believes that:										
... discussions between management and unions on alcohol or drug problems usually result in broad agreement	4	3				4	4	1		1
... a successful alcohol or drugs policy requires full consultation between management and unions	3	2	2	1		6	4			
... supervisors and managers usually do not have sufficient skills to identify alcohol or drug problems		7				3	5	2		
... management should take the lead to initiate policy on alcohol or drug problems	4	2			1	4	4	1	1	
... training for supervisors and managers is essential for an effective alcohol or drug policy		5	2			4	6			

V. Programmes in response to problems

A.   Overview

The view that the workplace is an essential factor regarding prevention efforts towards alcohol and drug abuse has become more and more dominant. As has been described in section II already, a movement has taken place within the last two or three years establishing alcohol as a topic of mutual concern between workers and employers. It was also mentioned that the responsible local authorities for prevention and treatment (the counties) to a high degree had included alcohol and work in their initiatives. There is no systematic knowledge of the specific content of the programmes established at the different workplaces, but a general trait seems to be that the enterprises enter into a co-operation with the community based counselling and treatment system. An aspect which has been debated recently is the workplace situation in relation to primary as well as secondary prevention on the background that the consumption of alcohol is no longer to any major extent workplace based. Though alcohol seems to be moving out of the workplace a high average consumption is still maintained in Denmark through a week-day evening and especially week-end consumption (see annex two table 1 and 4). Do the workplaces respond to an eventually high private but "visible" consumption with management/treatment programmes, even though the workplace has prohibition or regulation of alcohol consumption? The tendency seems to justify a yes.

As described in section I, the actions in relation to prevention are divided between the State and the regions (counties and municipalities), the State being responsible chiefly for general population campaigns and the regional authorities (through health, social, and educational boards) for activities directed towards specific target groups and the education-anchored prevention (accomplished in schools). Both levels of activities are organized thoroughly and run with regularity, being different in the regions according to the municipality decided priority, however (see also section II).

Regarding treatment and rehabilitation, a division exists also. The State being responsible for some psychiatric wards, and the counties for others together with alcohol clinics and rehabilitation centres. There is a tradition for a rather widespread activity from volunteer organizations in Denmark (as YMCA/YWCA, IOGT etc.). These organizations cooperate in close contact with the municipalities even undertaking treatment and rehabilitation supported by the municipalities. The volunteer-organizations are supported through the

State budget also for the time being a. 9 million Danish kroner (1.2 million ECU) and play a rather important role in advisory bodies at State and regional levels. A major tendency, within the last two-three years, has been a decentralization of the treatment/counselling/rehabilitation efforts establishing local centres responsible for a part of the county/municipality, at the same time establishing a more elaborate co-ordination at a central level. This process has not yet assumed its permanent form.

B.   Organizations and alcohol programmes

No programmes on prevention, treatment, training or rehabilitation are sponsored by employer's or by employee's organizations. One could say that until now the main effort from these organizations have been to support morally taking up the problems at enterprise level or to encourage it sometimes.

When regarding the organizations as a workplace in itself, very little seems to have been done to take up the question if an alcohol policy was appropriate. It seems, though, as if the trend in the ordinary workplace have provoked second thoughts in some of the organizations. The impression from a majority of the interviews was that it was considered to be a very difficult problem. But issuing of recommendations for a workplace alcohol policy from central organizational level, and a following up on these recommendations at branch or regional organizational level was expected to provoke a debate in the organization-workplace.

C.   Enterprises and Alcohol Programmes

Enterprises, having an alcohol policy, differ to a great degree regarding the implementation of this policy. In one extreme are enterprises which after having had the alcohol policy accepted in the joint industrial council do nothing but announce the policy to the employees. In the other extreme are enterprises which following the establishing of an alcohol policy set up a consultative body and support employees with problems financially, if they go into treatment. As an overview the picture below can be used.

1.   Establishment of an alcohol policy. No further initiatives.

2.   Establishment of an alcohol policy. Counselling with regard to public or private treatment/rehabilitation possibilities are provided. Initiative is up to the single employee otherwise.

3. Establishment of an alcohol policy. Internal Counselling is established arranging contact with treatment/rehabilitation institutions. If economy is necessary it is up to the single employee.

4. Establishment of an alcohol policy. Internal Counselling is established arranging contact with treatment/rehabilitation institutions. If economy is necessary the enterprise guarantees loan in bank or the like.

5. Establishment of an alcohol policy. Internal Counselling is established arranging contact with treatment/rehabilitation institutions. If economy is necessary the enterprise provides the means.

If the situation is of model 4 or 5, the enterprise will often give a substantial internal support using an alcohol consultant and/or establish informal or formal support for persons/groups among colleagues.

Across these different approaches there is the general denominator (except for the prohibitive enterprise) that periods of treatment and rehabilitation are considered as sick leave, and that employment security is part of the alcohol policy provided that the result of a treatment is controlled drinking or abstention from alcohol.

D.   Information and availability of assistance

Questions were raised to enterprises regarding responses to topics like prevention, assistance programmes, information procedures, etc. Table 16 presents the results on provision of information to employee or other prevention efforts.

Table 16: Information and training provided by enterprises

Information area	Alcohol	Drugs
Information to employees on effects and risks	6	2
Health promotion and other prevention activities	3	1
Training for supervisors on how to identify problems	3	1
Discussions to increase awareness of problem use at work	3	2

All enterprises have issued information about alcohol effects and risks from using alcohol to the employees except one, and three of the enterprises have established health promotion and prevention activities, discussions of the problems in using alcohol in the work situation, and training of leaders in problem-identification.

Enterprises are aware of the public health and social security system, and when appropriate, inform (councel) the employee. Self-help groups are included into this counselling also, but knowledge in the enterprises of other possibilities seems sparse. Internally, enterprise medical service and welfare counselling personnel and the shop steward system are acknowledged as existing possibilities. The shop stewards seem to be brought in nearly whenever problems arise for an employee. Medical sources and personnel counselling is used also, to a somewhat lesser degree, however, cf. tables 17 and 18.

Table 17: Internal resources for alcohol and drug prevention/treatment

Internal resource/unit	Available	Utilization in alcohol and drug cases				
		Never	Sometimes	Often	Always	Unsure
Medical department	6	2	3	1		
Personnel/welfare dept.	6	1	2	2	1	
Staff representative/Union ad-viser	7		1	5	1	
Specialist alcohol or drug unit						
Employee Assistance and Health Promotion Programme	1					1

Table 18: External resources for alcohol and drug prevention/treatment

External resource	Available	Utilization in alcohol and drug cases				
		Never	Sometimes	Often	Always	Unsure
Exployee Assistance and Health Promotion Programme	1	1	1			
State funded medical or social care facilities	5		2	3		
Insurance funded or fee-based treatment clinics	1		1			
Self-help groups (e.g. Alcoholics Anonymous)	4		2	1		1

In evaluating these results of questionnaires and interviews, it should be remembered that the number of employees with manifest alcohol problems are stated as very low by the enterprises. The percentage given ranged form 0.1% to 0.5% of the labour force in the enterprise, only one being at 0.5% the others either 0.1% and 0.2%.

E.   Drug Programmes

There is little information only relating to programmes of prevention regarding drugs. In interviews it was stated generally that drugs are no problem at all, and the existing knowledge, at the management level, covered a few isolated incidents of cannabis-use by apprentices. It was acknowledged, though, that there might be a hidden problem as the detection of a drug use could be more difficult than an alcohol abuse, if weak drugs (cannabis) or prescribed drugs were involved. Three enterprises state in the questionnaires that they are somewhat or much concerned about cannabis as a possible cause of workplace problems. But in no cases special initiatives/programmes were established for the drug area.

Respondents were aware that prescribed drugs were already or could become a problem. In several interviews one commented on the known high consumption of analgetica, anxiolytica and hypnotica in general in the Danish society. The possible effect of this use seems evident for the workplace. In the questionnaires four enterprises express concern about prescribed drugs as a possible cause of workplace problems.

VI. Cost of the problem and cost of responses

There was a unanimous answer from the enterprises regarding costs of alcohol related problems and responses to them. No one had produced special calculations in terms of budget. It was acknowledged that supposedly costs were involved having employees with a major alcohol consumption, but special figures had not been the foundation for discussions regarding an alcohol policy. The foundation for the discussion, previous to the introduction of an alcohol policy, had more been informal knowledge and impression of the situation of the enterprise supported by the general trends in the public debate of concern for the alcohol consumption in the population as such.

Regarding cost of responses as counselling service, treatment etc., nobody had calculated them, but a couple of enterprises stated that they were convinced it paid to have an alcohol policy and an assistance programme, the reasons given being different, however. In one case the costs of training the employees were so great that even a longer treatment were considered to pay off successfully. The other enterprise reasoned on the grounds that experience and group cohesion in the work process and in the workplace in general were considered to be very important, and "keeping the work force together" paid off.

At the national level, figures exist making estimations of the total cost of alcohol related problems in society. A figure of about six billion Danish kroner (equal to 750 million ECU) is often brought forward. In this figure the 2 billion kroner (250 million ECU) is the direct public   expenses on treatment and rehabilitation of people with alcohol related problems. The last 4 billion kroner (500 million ECU) is an estimate of what alcohol related problems cost in terms of loss in production caused by hangovers etc., forced pensions, children care, illness related to alcohol, alcohol related criminality etc. The criteria used for the estimates are very rough and imprecise, however.

Outside of strict budget considerations costs were commented on by several enterprises   implicitly stating that statistics of days lost through sickness (absence) seemed to indicate that the establishment of an alcohol policy had a general preventive effect. But no investigation seems to have been undertaken to prove the impression. Regarding cost related to accidents in the workplace neither enterprises nor organizations were of the impression that alcohol and drug played any significant role.

VII. Drug and alcohol testing and screening

In section 5 of the questionnaire and in the interview testing was defined as "... testing or screening of urine, blood or breath samples for the presence of drugs or alcohol ...". Except for the testing established by law, which takes place and is carried out by the police in case of accidents in certain sectors always, drug and alcohol testing and screening supposedly do not take place in Denmark. None of the enterprises participating had testing or screening programmes outside these lines and from the enterprises as well as the organizations there were in the interviews a clear NO to testing/screening along the defined lines. But two enterprises considered to have a testing procedure concerning alcohol and following accidents or incidents at work as required or following concerns or suspicion of individual employees. Both reactions came from the transport sector. The main pattern for the enterprises in statements on testing is: The enterprises *agree* or *strongly agree* in, that:

- the low prevalence of use does not justify testing,

- testing is an unacceptable intrusion on the private lives of job applicants and employees,

- testing represents an unacceptable change to employees' terms and conditions of work,

- implementation of testing procedures is too costly.

The enterprises on the other hand *disagree* or *strongly disagree* in the fact that:

- testing is the only objective measure available to detect problems of alcohol or drug use,

- pre-employment testing has a positive role in deterring problem drug and alcohol users from applying to organizations.

On the other items presented in the questionnaire (q. 22) the response patterns are more diffuse.

Table 19: Attitude to testing/screening

Item	Enterprises						Organizations					
	Strongly agree	Agree	Disagree	Strongly disagree	Unsure	No answer	Strongly agree	Agree	Disagree	Strongly disagree	Unsure	No answer
.. implementing a testing programme is too costly of financial and other resources	3	3			1			3	1	1	4	1
... testing is the only objective measure available to detect problem alcohol or drug use	3		3	1				2	4	3	1	
... positive test results do not provide evidence of impaired work performance		2	2	1	2		1	4	3	1	1	
... testing is not a valid or reliable measure of the extent of problem drug or alcohol use in the workplace	2	2	2	1			2	4	2	1	1	
... testing is an unacceptable intrusion into the private lives of job applicants and/or employees	3	2			1	1	5	2	1	1		1
... Testing should be limited to employees who work in safety sensitive jobs		2		2	3		1	6	2		1	
... the low prevalence of drug and alcohol use in the workplace does not justify the implementation of a testing policy	3	2	1		1		3	3	2		1	
... testing is valuable, but only as part of a wider programme of employee assistance and health promotion		2	1	2	2		1	2	2	3	1	1
... pre-employment testing has a positive role in deterring problem drug and alcohol users from applying to organizations			2	3	2		1	1	4	2	2	
...testing represents an unacceptable change to employees' terms and conditions of work	3	3			1		4	4		1	1	

VIII.   Information availability and exchange

Information on alcohol and drug problems were considered important by all participants. At organizational level a few initiatives has been taken in systematically gathering information, the first result being a joint publication from the Confederation of Employers and the Confederation of Trade Unions (Grunnet & Bang, 1991). The information on the extent of problems or other statistics relating to alcohol and drugs have not been elaborated on by any organization. Information does exist at different levels concerning consumption, problems etc. in the workplace, but as part of research data as for example presented by Colling (1988) and Sabroe (1989). These data have to a certain degree been used in the debate between employers and employees, especially at organizational level.

At the enterprise level information is accumulated to a minor degree in three of the enterprises regarding the extent of problems and of work problems related to alcohol or drug use primarily. The information was informal and not available for official use or publication, however.

Ranking subjects considered to be most important, a rather dissimilar picture appears. All five subjects presented get low and high ranking. In average the enterprise and organizational ranking is as follows:

Table 20: Information topics ranked by organizations and enterprises

Information content	Organizations	Enterprises
1. The effectiveness of workplace programmes	1	4
2. Extent of alcohol and drug related problems in the workplace	3	1=2
3. Workplace responses in other organizations and countries	5	5
4. Costs of problems	4	2=1
5. Approaches and techniques for prevention	2	3

IX. Outlook and opinion

An overwhelming impression from interview as well as questionnaire data is one of an extensive degree of harmony in the opinions on alcohol and drugs in general and alcohol and drugs in the workplace in special. This unison can be described by the following, the word agreement used for a clear majority view and comes out as follows:

1. There is an agreement that there is a high level of alcohol consumption in Denmark in general, and that illegal drugs are an existing problem, mostly confined to marginal groups, however. The general consumption of prescribed drugs is relatively high, also.

2. There is an agreement that drugs are an extremely small workplace problem verging on non-existent.

3. There is an agreement that alcohol and drug policies in the workplace are a good thing, that they should be established through negotiations between employers and employees, and that these negotiations are successful generally.

4. There is an agreement that the actual incidence of workplace problems related to alcohol and drugs is low, but there is some concern about alcohol and prescribed drugs nevertheless.

5. There is an agreement that prevention of alcohol or drug related work problems should be given high priority.

6. There is an agreement that a case to case approach based on individual circumstances should be used when problems appear.

7. There is an agreement that testing and screening in general are incompatible with the Danish attitude to the individual and his/her integrity as a person. Presented with specific questions there is an opinion that anyway incidences are too small to justify testing, and that testing is too costly.

8. There is agreement that the enterprise has the responsibility to support treatment and rehabilitation of employees if they run into troubles, and at the same time a belief that employees respond well to management and/or treatment, and that it pays to have these programmes.

Having presented this agreement picture, it is necessary to say that there are differences in opinions across the organizations and enterprises participating in the project, but that they more could be regarded as exceptions compared to the agreements.

One sign of the agreement is the joint products from the Employers' Confederation and the Confederation of Trade Unions. In the first one a conclusion is drawn on the basis of presentations at a seminar for major Danish enterprises, union and municipality representatives established by the two confederations and the Health Council of Copenhagen (Grunnet and Bang, 1990, p. 123):

> A social problem of abuse exists, including alcohol abuse.
>
> The exposed age group is the 20-50-year-olds. These are generally in employment and "in good health" and have little contact with the health system or social service authorities.
>
> The abuse affects the individual's health and well-being as well as the efficiency of the enterprise, in which he is employed.
>
> The workplace is the natural starting point for efforts trying to solve personal problems relating to abuse.

The conference came up with two recommendations (ibid. p. 123-126):

1. "Don't consider a person's drink problems a taboo. You solve no problems, neither those of the employee nor those of the enterprise closing your eyes".."

2. "Make it clear to the staff that to deal with alcohol problems constitutes an integrated part of an overall personnel policy - no more no less."

Further work in the Main Joint Industrial Council has resulted in a joint publication with four recommendations and eight subjects for discussion (DA/LO, 1992). Of the four recommendations the two first are overlapping the just mentioned. The two supplementary are:

3. "The Joint Industrial Council should discuss and suggest rules for alcohol, to be implemented as part of prevention, treatment and disciplinary

reactions. Rules should include availability of alcohol (in the enterprise). It is important to have a clear alcohol policy, known by and common for all in the workplace."

4. "Be aware of the early signals from a (potential) alcohol dependent." (Changed slightly in the translation by K-E. S.)

When looking at a special area as alcohol and drugs in the workplace, it is always important to realize how this topic is anchored in the general culture relating to the area. It is obvious that the liberal attitude towards alcohol in society, which is prevailing in Denmark, will be a frame to consider when for example trying to establish an alcohol policy. The impact from this liberal attitude has been very different across the participating enterprises/organizations. But the major impression is that a majority finds the liberal attitude should be present in the workplace alcohol policies also, and that prohibition is not a way compatible with Danish culture. On the other hand, research results seem to indicate that this cultural perspective might be changing and restrictions and control in some form being more acceptable (Sabroe, 1991, 1994). The preceding three decades have proven that the Danish alcohol culture by no means is static.

References

Aarhus Amtskommune (1988): *Forsøgsprojekt alkohol og arbejdsmiljø.* Aarhus: Amtskommunen, mimeo, 63 p. ("Alcohol and Working Conditions").

Bunnage, D. (red.) (1992): *Levevilkår i Danmark.* København: Socialforskningsinstituttet. ("Life conditions in Denmark").

Colling, Hanne (1988) *Alkohol og arbejdsliv.* København: Socialforskningsinstituttet ("Alcohol and work life").

Colling, Hanne (1991): *Tøbrud i den danske debat om alkohol på arbejdspladsen.* In: Nordisk Alkohol Tidsskrift, 8, 1991, 2. ("Thaw in the Danish debate on alcohol in the workplace").

DA/LO 1992: *Forslag til alkoholpolitik på arbejdspladsen.* Copenhagen: DA/LO. ("Recommendations for an Alcohol Policy at the Workplace").

DA (Dansk Arbejdsgiverforening) (1992) DA-miljø 43/92. København: Dansk Arbejdsgiverforening ("Pamphlet on survey results").

Danmarks Statistik: Ti-års oversigt 1983-93. København: Danmarks Statistik. ("Statistics. Ten years overview").

Folketingsforhandlinger (1979): *Forespørgsel vedrørende narkotikamisbruget 29.11.1979.* ("Danish Parliament debate").

Grant, M. (Ed.) (1985). *Alcohol policies.* Copenhagen: WHO.

Grunnet, K. & Bang, H.-J. (eds.) (1990): *Alkohol og medarbejderudvikling.* København: Dansk Arbejdsgiverforening. ("Alcohol and Employee Development").

Grunnet, K. (1990): *Alkohol og personalepolitik.* København: Dansk Arbejdsgiverforening. ("Alcohol and Personnel Policy").

Hansen, E.J. & Andersen, D. (1985): *Alkoholforbrug og alkoholpolitik.* København: Socialforskningsinstituttet. ("Alcohol Consumption and Alcohol Policy").

Larsen, Ester (1991): *Arbejdsgiveren* J, 1991 (4. February).

Leroy, B. (1991). *Medicine and health*. Brussels: Commission of the European Community.

Milhøj, A. (1993): Virkningen af afgiftsindsættelserne på øl og vinsalget i Danmark. *Nordisk Alkohol Tidsskrift*, vol. 10, no. 6. ("The impact of excise reduction on the sale of alcohol in Denmark").

NAT (Nordisk Alkohol Tidsskrift) (1992): *Ökad dansk alkoholmedvetenhet*. NAT 9, pp. 280-283. ("Increased Danish Alcohol Consciousness").

Nielsen, Kirsten (1982): *Danskernes alkoholvaner*. København: Alkohol og Narkotikarådet ("Danish alcohol habits").

Nøgletal om udviklingen i sygdom og sundhed (1992). København: Forebyggelsespolitisk Råd. ("Central figures on the development of health and sickness").

Politiets Årsberetning 1993. ("Police annual report 1993").

Rasmussen, O. & Sabroe, K.-E. (1989): Frequency Tables. Aarhus: Institute of Psychology.

Sabroe, K.-E. (1991): Alkoholforbrug. *Udviklingstendenser 1988-90*. In: Petersen, E. et al. *De trivsomme og arbejdsomme danskere*. Aarhus: Aarhus Universitetsforlag ("Alcohol Consumption. Development Tendencies 1988-90").

Sabroe, K.-E. (1994): Alcohol and work. In: Sabroe, K.-E. *Alcohol in society*. Aarhus: Aarhus University Press.

Sabroe, K.-E. & Laursen, L. (1994): Preliminary results from survey. Internal report (unpublished).

Statistisk Årbog 1992. København: Danmarks Statistik. ("Danish Statistics 1992").

Statistisk Årbog 1994. København: Danmarks Statistik. ("Danish Statistics 1994").

Sundhedsministeriet (1991): Alkoholpolitik i en nøddeskal. Købehavn: Sundhedsministeriet. ("Alcohol policy in a nut shell").

Sundhedsstyrelsen (1991): *Alkohol- og narkotikamisbruget 1985-89.* København: Statens Information. ("Alcohol and Narcotics Abuse 1985-89").

Sundhedsstyrelsen (1992): *Alkohol- og narkotikamisbruget 1990-91.* København: Statens Information. ("Alcohol and Narcotics Abuse 1990-91").

Sælan, H (1985): *Alkohol og arbejdsliv.* In: Alkoholdebat no. 20. ("Alcohol and work-life").

Thorsen, T. (1988): *Danskerne drikker mere end som så.* A & N Debat, 33, pp. 16-21. (The Danes Drink More than one Think").

Thorsen, T. (1990): *Hundrede års alkoholmisbrug.* København: Alkohol og Narkotikarådet. ("A hundred years of alcohol abuse").

Mam....ittqut... (........) Ai....q......... ....q...
.....l..   .....u..   ....l..   ...q.   .....

....
....

....
....

....
....

....
...n...   T.....q...............   ....

....
....

Annex one

The transport sector. A profile

I. Policy and organizational aspects

In arranging the population the *transport sector* was given special attention. At the enterprise level participation was covering as well air, as sea and land transport being at a national and local level, and comprising a total of about 30.000 employers in three enterprises. At the organizational level one national organization covering the specific sector participated. At the union level transport workers were part of more unions, but it was not possible to seperate them in the results.

In a broad view, the main impression is that very *great overlap* existed in response to the different topics raised in the questionnaire and the interviews. All the *enterprises* have a written alcohol policy, and two enterprises have also taken up drugs in policy statements, drugs were not considered to be any problem, though. On the other hand concern was expressed regarding prescribed medicine. The alcohol policies had been in effect for between 2 and 12 years.

At national organization level no general written policy had been established, but information existed that several *sub-organizations* had a formal alcohol policy.

II. Worker - employer relations

Establishing an *alcohol policy* had been a result of *negotiations* between employers and employees in all cases, and though diverse opinions had been expressed no conflict had been the result. When a policy is institutionalized it is widely distributed through several channels including personal copy to employees.

III. Nature, trend and extent of problems. Costs

Regarding the *nature of alcohol and drug problems* in the workplace neither the enterprises nor organization indicate an "often" response to the different work problems presented. For *drug* problems the nearly unanimous response was a "never" to the question of having experienced problems among

67

members/employees. One enterprise gave the response "sometimes" to most kinds of work problems regarding drugs, though. But it should be added that during the interview the participants expressed that "sometimes" was experienced as also covering very rare occasions and in the actual case it was more an expression covering an evaluation of a possibility based on knowledge of very few cases. For *alcohol* somewhat more responses were in the "sometimes" category. For the work problems of "damage to equipment/property" and "theft of company property" the response from all were "never".

Seemingly, there is very little concrete knowledge of an *increase or decrease of alcohol and drug problems*. Most reactions were "unsure", but answers given in the interviews give the impression that alcohol problems are decreasing. Regarding the present situation, and irrespective of the stated impression of alcohol problems as decreasing, it is expressed that one is "somewhat concerned" about alcohol as a potential cause of work related problems in general, and prescribed drugs are also brought forward. But for illegal drugs an "unsure" reaction is the general response.

The transport sector representatives *disagree* or strongly disagree with the assumption that they should have *more members with alcohol or drug problems* than other organizations/sectors. But they are aware that the work in the sector could be *seriously affected* by alcohol or drug use and that it could cause a significant *rising in costs*. As a result - one could say - they have given high priority to the *prevention* of alcohol and drug use affecting the workplace. There is in the transport sector some differences in opinion regarding the question if *work demands* in the transport sector work contribute to the development of alcohol or drug problems, but reactions on the topic are not strong.

IV. Information availability and exchange

Until the present no initiatives have been taken from any of the enterprises or organizations regarding systematic collection of *information* about alcohol or drug problems. For some problems it was possible for the enterprises to deduce information from general figures of alcohol and work related problems. One could get the impression from the interviews, not explicitly stated although, that the accentuation being a potential result of surveys and statistical elaboration of specific organizational figures or alike would bring the topic of alcohol and drug problems in an inconvenient placing, and maybe influence the seemingly positive spirit in which the establishment and implementation of an alcohol policy had taken place. One enterprise clearly gave this as a reason to refuse participating in the present project. All participating enterprises/organizations express that *discussions* between management and union are fruitful and always end in a *satisfactory* agreement, and also that such discussions are a *necessity*.

Asked about the priority given to topics considered important for information a very diffuse picture is the result. The only vague trends are that one agrees, to a certain extent, that information about the effectiveness of workplace programmes has low priority and that cost and benefits of policy and assistance programmes have high priority.

The topic of especially alcohol problems and the work has been an issue for all enterprises/organizations in local newsletters or similar, but two enterprises had carried out deliberate *campaigns*. Two of the enterprises also emphasized that materials from national campaigns had been made available for the employees. *Research* initiatives have not been initiated by enterprises in the transport sector or by organizations of the sector.

V. Programmes in response to problems

The representatives agree that *supervisors and management* do not have sufficient *skills* to identify alcohol or drug problems, and that *training* is mandatory for a successful implementation of an alcohol/drug policy. No one had established such training as yet.

Two enterprises had a special *consultant on alcohol* and drug problems, cooperating with medical services, personal consultants in general and the shop-steward system. In no cases one had a complete *internal* programme with prevention, treatment and rehabilitation. The consultant and the belonging staff took care of prevention initiatives and information and acted as "visitator" regarding employees with alcohol (drug) problems to relevant *external* institutions. In some cases the enterprises backed an employee referred to treatment financially, in other cases the costs were an employee matter, but the enterprise guaranteed for loan if necessary. In case of treatment at an institution, the treatment period was registered as (normal) sick leave. These last pieces of information lead to the ascertainment, that all enterprises/organizations state that they find a *case by case approach* based on individual circumstances most relevant for alcohol/drug problems, one enterprise indicating that disciplinary reactions could be necessary. The *amount of employees* considered *having an alcohol problem* is stated as very low (0.1%), only one enterprise considers a figure for drug problems being 0.02% of the employees.

Taking *reactions on treatment efforts*, the trend is that one believe in positive response to treatment from employees/members, and also that the employees being treated for alcohol problems are able to *recover* and *resume work* effectively. Further the opinion is that the enterprise has a responsibility to support an employee's treatment and that an enterprise assistance should be available besides resources provided by the state.

VI. Testing and screening

No *testing* programme is established in the sector except the by law demanded in case of accidents and the by law demanded medical examinations for air-craft crews as an example. There are no intentions of establishing testing procedures using blood or urine samples, neither for applicants nor for employees in the participating enterprises/organizations, outside the above indicated. *Specific reactions* to the raised questions on testing in the project display a rather great spread, but some dominating trends are: that testing is too costly, that testing is an unacceptable intrusion into private life, that the low prevalence of alcohol and drug use in the workplace does not justify implementation of testing and that testing represents an unacceptable change to employee's terms and conditions of work.

Conclusion

No great surprises appear comparing the transport sector picture with the labour market picture in general. The main tendencies are present in equal degree, indicating an openness towards the problems of alcohol and drugs. These tendencies give the impression also that until recently very little has been done to ascertain if the calm-sea picture presented is valid. Movements though have taken place, lately being supported by the main employers' and employees' confederations, to ensure that a formulated alcohol policy becomes an integrative part of the organizational pattern of any enterprise. The experience of already established and implemented alcohol and drug policies is very positive in enterprises and a considerable preventive effect is claimed to be the result from these policies.

In general the participating transport sector enterprises present a picture of: very low amount of actual problems; not concerned about drugs as work related problems, but concerned about alcohol problems somewhat although they are decreasing; agreement on negotiations between employers and employees as a necessity; supervisors and management not able to diagnose problems and training therefore necessary; information about alcohol and drug problems are communicated but research is not initiated; the preferred approach to problems is case by case and individual oriented, and there is an acceptance of enterprise responsibility in supporting treatment and rehabilitation; one is opposed to testing both for applicants and employees.

Annex Two

Alcohol patterns of the Danish population

Below is presented information on the quantitative distribution of the alcohol consumption in Denmark according to time of day, day of week, gender, age, and type of alcohol.

The reason to present this more general information, especially concerning the alcohol consumption situation, is that it is felt necessary to understand the results in the country report. These results are from a major survey carried out in 1989 and supported by results from minor surveys in 1988 and 1990 (Sabroe, 1991, 1994). The seven graphs highlight the Danish alcohol consumption pattern in general. As seen on p. 20, the Danish alcohol consumption has in the late eighties and the early nineties been slightly declining after having flattened off since the early seventies on the top of a steep rise in the preceding twenty years. A rise in 1992 and supposedly also in 1993 has caused some concern, however, and figures from the first two quarters of 1994 seem to indicate a sale bringing the average consumption still higher up.

In the first graph is illustrated how the Danes distribute their consumption through the 24 hours. With working hours normally being between 7 and 16, it is obvious that only a very minor part of the Danes consume alcohol during this period and it should be remembered that the population in the graphs is from a survey with a representative sample, thus including pensioners, unemployed, etc. The peak consumption hours are at 12 and 18, the times when the Danes have lunch and dinner. Looking at the amount-distribution in the second graph it also proves that the amount drunk in this period is small, relatively seen. As illustrated in the third graph, beer and wine show a similar picture in the day distribution, spirits having a somewhat dissimilar pattern.

Fig 1: Alcohol consumption (in total)
over 24 hours

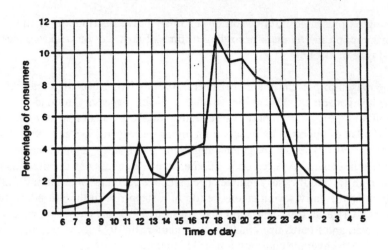

Fig. 2: Average amount consumed
over 24 hours

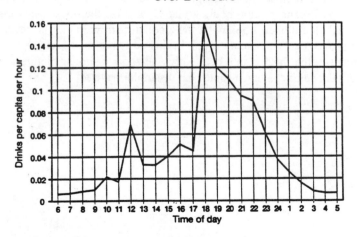

Fig. 3: Consumption (types of alcohol)
distribution over 24 hours

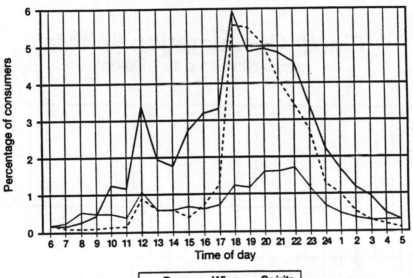

Seen over the week, the fourth graph again proves that it is not during the work-days we have the major consumption evidently. It is in the leisure time, in the weekends, and at home the Danes have their relatively high consumption. If we again look at the types of alcohol as in the fifth graph, the same similarity for wine and beer as in the day picture appears in the week picture. This day and week picture is the result of a development over a period, in which the amount of alcohol consumed not is reduced to any major extent but in which a replacement of the situations it is consumed have taken place. From survey results it was assumed that between 30-35% of all alcohol was drunk at the workplace around 1980.

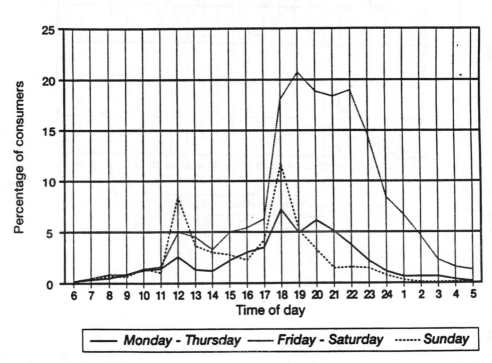

Fig. 4: Consumption (in total)
according to day of week

Fig. 5: Consumption (type of alcohol)
distribution over the week

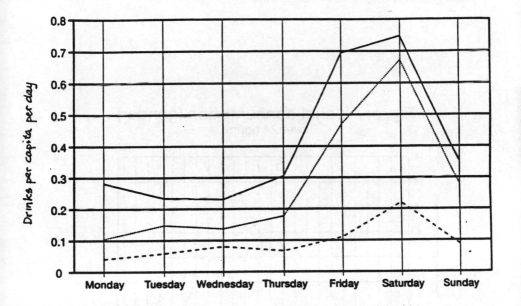

Considering person characteristics as in figure 6, one finds that men and women at their different levels display a similar picture, regarding our interest area of the workplace, however, it should be noted that whereas the amount of women having alcohol at work is reduced after lunch, the men keep the level and even raise it around closing time. Regarding age, we get an interesting pattern in figure 7. The middle and elderly people display the same "two peak picture" as obtained in the general data, for the elder the picture of meal-connected drinking is even more pronounced. For the younger the meal connection is not apparent, the peak is two hours later and consumption during the work day is clearly smaller than for the two age groups.

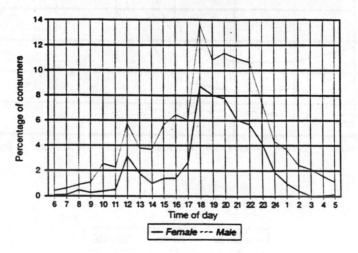

Fig. 6: Alcohol consumption (gender)
over 24 hours

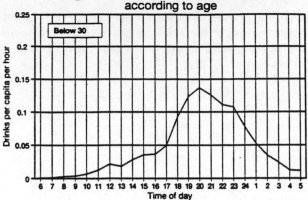

Fig. 7A: Alcohol consumption
according to age

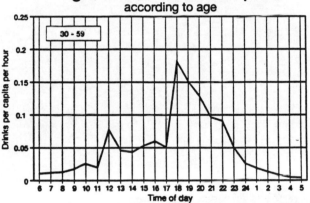

Fig. 7B: Alcohol consumption
according to age

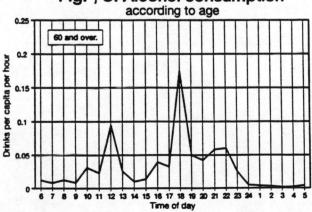

Fig. 7C: Alcohol consumption
according to age

79

I shall not go into a wider discussion at this time, but it is obvious that the general picture shown in the seven graphs is important to understand the situation and the movements regarding alcohol in the workplace.

Annex Three

Data on Alcohol and Work

(Tables from Sabroe (1994): Alcohol and work)

Table 1: Alcohol consumption in the workplace

Frequency	Total %	Sex	
		Women %	Men %
1 Daily	3.9	0.3	7.5
2 A couple of times/week	5.4	1.3	9.5
3 One time/week	7.1	4.0	10.2
4 A couple of times/month	6.2	3.9	8.5
5 One time/month	5.1	.5.1	5.0
6 A couple of times/year	4.7	5.9	3.6
7 One time/year	1.6	1.8	1.4
8 Only special occasions	13.9	15.8	12.1
9 Never	49.2	59.3	39.5
10 Alcohol prohibition	2.0	1.5	2.4
11 Don't know	.8	1.0	.5
12 Refuse to answer	0.1	0.1	0
N = 2001	100	51.3	48.7

Table 2: Alcohol consumption in the workplace according to age (percentage)

	alcohol prohib.	daily	cpl. times/ week	one time/ week.	cpl. times/ mth.	one time/ mth.	cpl. times/ year	one time year	only special occ.	never	don't know	no answer	Total
15-19	4.2	1.0	2.1	6.3			3.1		10.4	72.9			6.1
20-29	1.7	2.3	6.6	11.7	6.3	7.1	6.3	1.4	10.3	46.2	0.3		22.2
30-39	2.5	4.2	7.2	8.0	9.0	5.5	4.2	1.7	14.0	42.6	.7	.2	25.4
40-49	1.7	5.0	5.2	5.2	6.9	6.9	5.2	2.5	17.1	43.1	1.1		22.9
50-59	2.2	6.0	3.0	4.3	5.2	3.4	3.0	0.9	16.4	54.7	0.9		14.7
60-69		3.5	5.3	3.5	1.8		6.2	1.8	13.3	63.7	0.9		7.2
70-89				4.0	4.0				12.0	76.0	4.0		1.6
Total	2.0	3.9	5.4	7.2	6.2	5.1	4.7	1.6	13.9	49.2	0.8	0.1	100.0

Table 3: Alcohol consumption in the workplace according to occupation (percentage)

	alcohol prohib.	daily	cpl. times/ week	one time/ week	cpl. times/ month	one time/ month	cpl. times/ year	one time/ year	only special occ.	never	don't know	no answer	Total
Skilled worker	1.4	10.1	8.0	11.2	8.0	5.4	4.3	2.2	10.9	38.4			17.4
Independent	2.0	6.1	5.1	3.1	4.1	2.0	4.1	2.0	13.3	56.1	2.0		6.2
Unskilled worker	3.1	3.5	3.9	3.9	5.0	4.2	6.9	1.2	12.4	55.2	0.8		16.4
Farmer (indep.)		2.7	8.1	8.1		2.7	2.7		8.1	64.9	2.7		2.3
Employee/civil serv.	1.5	2.6	6.8	6.6	8.2	6.8	5.1	1.4	18.2	42.4	0.3		41.0
Appren./stud./pupil.	3.6	.5	.5	10.7	3.1	3.6	3.6	2.0	10.7	60.7	.5	.5	12.4
Helpmate			3.8	7.7				3.8	3.8	73.1	7.7		1.6
Housewife									6.5	90.3	3.2		2.0
Refuse to answer										90.9	9.1		.7
Total	2.0	3.9	5.4	7.1	6.2	5.1	4.7	1.6	13.9	49.2	.8	.1	100.0

Table 4: Access to alcohol in the workplace according to occupation (percentage)

	Free access	Limited access	No access	No answer	No answer	Total
Skilled worker	14.6	42.5	36.4	6.4		14.0
Employee/civil serv.	10.2	52.5	32.0	4.5	0.8	32.5
Independent	9.1	42.4	42.4	5.1	1.0	4.9
Unskilled worker	8.0	43.1	45.0	3.8		13.0
Unempl./pensioners/early retired	5.8	37.4	49.2	7.6		19.0
Appren./stud./pupil	5.4	55.1	34.6	4.9		10.2
Farmer	5.3	39.5	50.0	5.3		1.9
Housewife	4.4	17.8	75.6	2.2		2.2
Helpmate		37.9	62.1			1.4
Refuse to answer	16.7	41.7	41.7			.6
Total	8.8	45.5	40.2	5.2	.3	100.0

Table 5: Work colleagues with a high alcohol consumption according to occupation (percentage)

	Yes	No	Don't know	No answer	Total
Skilled worker	62.5	36.8	.4	.4	14.0
Employee/civil serv.	61.0	38.4	0.6		32.5
Unskilled worker	53.8	45.0	1.2		13.0
Independent	50.5	46.5	3.0		4.9
Unemployed	39.7	54.7	5.3	.3	19.0
Appren./stud./pupil	38.5	54.6	6.8		10.2
Helpmate	34.5	58.6	6.9		1.4
Farmer	13.2	78.9	7.9		1.9
Housewife	11.1	71.1	15.6	2.2	2.2
Refuse to answer	25.0	75.0			.6
Total	50.8	46.2	2.8	.1	⁻ 100.0

Annex four

Tables from National report on the drug abuse situation
(Pompidou group paper, 1991, and Danish Health Council, 1993)

Table 1: Seizures of drugs 1986-1992 in kg

Drug	1986	1988	1989	1992
Heroin	17.3	29.2	37.7	39.5
Cocaine	7.1	9.7	54.9	21.4
Amphetamines	10.2	29.8	25.0	73.6
Cannabis	472.0	1,369.3	729.0	2,152.0
Hemp grown in Denmark	1,664.7	8,636.0	2,372.0	9,209.0

Table 2: Charges of drug-related crime

Legal Title	1986 number	1988 number	1989 number	1992 number
Section 191(1) of the Danish Criminal Code (sale)	1,062	1,415	1,155	603
Section 191(2) of the Danish Criminal Code (smuggling)	552	645	574	267
Section 191(a) of the Danish Criminal Code (receiving stolen goods)	21	80	42	33
The Euphoriant Substances act	8,016	11,886	13,039	16,379
Total numbers of charges	9,651	14,026	14,810	17,282

Table 3: Drugs and drug use

Percentage of adults (above the age of 14) tried drugs

Drug	Ever tried	Tried within last 12 months
Cannabis	22%	5%
Amphetamines	3%	1%
Cocaine	1%	0.2%
Heroin	0.1%	0.1%

Table 4: Drugs and treatment (number treated per year)

Year	Number treated
1985	2,826
1986	3,166
1987	2,877
1988	2,912
1989	3,326
1990	3,629
1991	3,821
Male/female ratio approx.	3/1

Table 5: Drugs and death

Year	Drug related death
1985	150
1986	109
1987	140
1988	135
1989	135
1992	208

Annex five

Alcohol-related Problems

(Table source: Danish Health Council)

Table 1: Treatment in wards and alcohol clinics

Year	Somatic wards number of charges	Psychiatric wards number of admission	Alcohol clinics number of treatments
1985	12,941	13,878	17,680
1986	14,082	13,181	18,126
1987	13,291	11,867	17,250
1988	13,498	11,248	17,477
1989	14,172	10,198	16,560
1990	14,283	9,929	-
1991	14,494	8,837	-
1992	-	8,448	-
Male/female ratio average	70/30	68/32	72/28

Table 2: Alcohol related death (inhabitants above 14)

	Diagnoses				
Year	Alcoholism	Liver cirrhosis	Pancreatitis	Alcohol poisoning	Alcohol psychosis
1985	150	641	89	46	3
1986	122	687	88	46	1
1987	133	701	83	44	2
1988	196	658	73	45	2
1989	222	726	84	36	3
1990	255	712	80	54	1
1991	245	718	88	47	5

Table 3: Alcohol and traffic

Year	Number of traffic accidents with person damage	Percentage of total accidents
1985	2,403	21.1
1986	2,278	20.4
1987	2,054	20.2
1988	1,929	19.3
1989	1,975	19.9
1990	1,613	17.6
1991	1,491	17.0
1992	1,534	17.1

Annex six

Facts on alcohol and drug misuse in Denmark

(Source: Danish Health Council)

Alcohol:

1. Seventy out of hundred are considered to have an umpromatic relation to alcohol.

2. Seventyfour out of hundred are having an overconsumption.

3. Six out of hundred have an alcohol consumption at a level of potential health risk.

4. Seven males out of ten have alcohol abuse problems in violence affected families.

5. Five out of ten children, being placed in foster families or children's institutions, come from families, in which alcohol abuse is part of the problem.

6. A total of 100 children, out of 46,000 births a year are born with damages caused by alcohol.

7. Five out of ten convicted to jail are in need for alcohol treatment.

Drugs:

1. The number of drug addicts is estimated to be about 10.000.

2. Drug addicts have an over-death rate of twenty times.

3. Drug addicts constitute 27% of all committed to prison.

4. One out of six intravenous drug addicts is below the age of 25.

5. The number of children with drug addict parents are increasing.

English resume of "subject-sheet no. 9" from the Danish Health Council (issued as part of national campaign).

Alcohol and Work (Information and suggestions)

1. An increasing number of enterprises has established an alcohol policy as part of the general personnel policy. Employees are beginning to consider alcohol policy as part of good working conditions.

2. A debate on alcohol problems ought to be initiated in the workplace, this being an important forum for discussions and opinion-formation.

3. Investigations prove that alcohol is not a major problem in the workplace. Less than 4% have alcohol at work daily. A majority of the population finds that alcohol should be prohibited or restricted in the workplace.

4. Aims of an alcohol policy should include:
    - Remove the taboo around alcohol
    - Open discussions of our high national consumption
    - Establish frames for consumption, ensuring that a drink pressure does not exist
    - Establish possibilities for treatment of employees with high consumption of alcohol in preference to dismissal.

5. Rules for alcohol consumption in the enterprises (examples):
    - Restrictions on *when* to drink alcohol
    - Restrictions on *where* to drink alcohol
    - Restrictions on *how much* to drink
    - Restrictions for special employee groups
    - Restrictions for all inclusive management

6. Sanctions most often seem to be verbal appeal in different degrees followed by dismissal, if not respected.

7. Prevention and treatment have been mainly two types
    - Individual oriented
    - Collective oriented meaning that a colleague or a colleague group have been involved in the process.

INSTRUKTIONER TIL FORFATTERE

Forfattere, der ønsker at sende bidrag til skriftserien, skal følge de nedenfor nævnte retningslinier mht. udformning af artikler:

1. Hvis artiklerne skrives på en IBM-kompatibel PC i enten WordPerfect eller Word, sendes en diskette med artiklen til redaktionen. Artiklen skal sendes som en ASCII fil.

2. Al tekst skal starte ved venstre margin og have ujævn højre margin.

3. For Word-brugere skal teksten skrives uden tomme linier ved nyt afsnit.

4. Fodnoter skrives med normal skrifttype til sidst i artiklen.

5. Udover disketten sendes artiklen udprintet med de formatteringer, dvs. understregninger, kursiv, fede typer, store typer m.m., der ønskes.

6. Tabeller og figurer vedlægges på papir.

7. Hvis man ikke kan skrive i enten WordPerfect eller i Word, kan man sende artiklen maskinskrevet.

8. Litteratur- og referenceliste skrives altid til sidst i manus.

9. Henvisninger i teksten til referencelisten skal have formen: (Forfatter, årstal), f.eks. (Goldman, 197).

Med venlig hilsen

Redaktionen